dear Sarah

Letters Home from a Soldier of the Iron Brigade

INDIANA UNIVERSITY PRESS

BLOOMINGTON & INDIANAPOLIS

dear Sarah

EDITED BY CORALOU PEEL LASSEN

THIS BOOK IS A PUBLICATION OF
INDIANA UNIVERSITY PRESS
601 NORTH MORTON STREET
BLOOMINGTON, INDIANA 47404-3797 USA

WWW.INDIANA.EDU/~IUPRESS

Telephone orders   800-842-6796
Fax orders   812-855-7931
Orders by email   IUPORDER@INDIANA.EDU

LIBRARY OF CONGRESS CATALOGING-IN-PUBLICATION DATA

PARDINGTON, JOHN HENRY, D. 1863
DEAR SARAH: LETTERS HOME FROM A SOLDIER OF THE IRON BRIGADE /
EDITED BY CORALOU PEEL LASSEN.
P.   CM.
INCLUDES BIBLIOGRAPHICAL REFERENCES (P.   ) AND INDEX.
ISBN 0-253-33560-4 (ALK. PAPER)
1. PARDINGTON, JOHN HENRY, D. 1863—CORRESPONDENCE. 2. UNITED STATES. ARMY. MICHIGAN
INFANTRY REGIMENT, 24TH (1862–1865) 3. UNITED STATES. ARMY. IRON BRIGADE (1861–1865) 4.
MICHIGAN—HISTORY—CIVIL WAR, 1861–1865—PERSONAL NARRATIVES. 5. UNITED STATES—
HISTORY—CIVIL WAR, 1861–1865—PERSONAL NARRATIVES. 6. MICHIGAN—HISTORY—CIVIL WAR,
1861–1865—REGIMENTAL HISTORIES. 7. UNITED STATES—HISTORY—CIVIL WAR, 1861–1865—
REGIMENTAL HISTORIES. 8. SOLDIERS—MICHIGAN—CORRESPONDENCE.   I. LASSEN, CORALOU
PEEL, DATE.   II. TITLE.
E514.5 24TH.P37   1999
973.7'474—DC21   98-56077

1   2   3   4   5   04   03   02   01   00   99

To *John Henry Pardington*,

with deepest gratitude,
for reminding us that
wars are fought by real
people—folks with
dreams and heart-
aches—and for
rekindling the spark
of patriotism lying
dormant within many
hearts.

Contents

dear Sarah

Illustrations

Maps

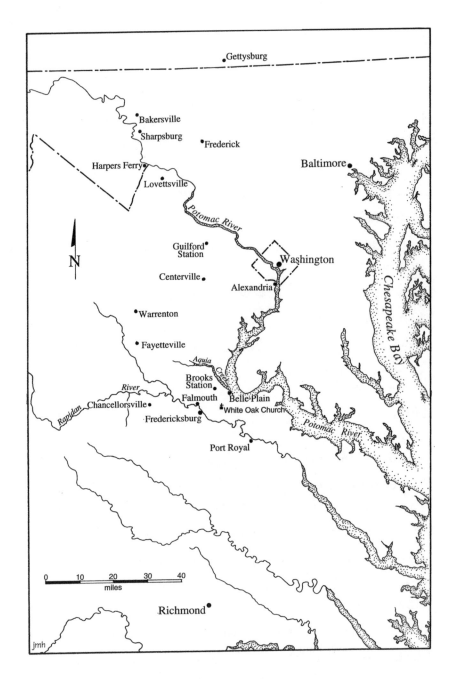

Virginia, Maryland, and Pennsylvania

Acknowledgments

The project of editing these letters over the past several years has been wonderfully rewarding. In many ways, I am saddened to see it come to an end, because it has provided much interest, knowledge, fun, and enlightenment to my life.

I am deeply grateful to my close friends, relatives, and acquaintances who have encouraged me and helped me along the way. Some of them deserve special mention: Renee Doxsee for helping me with the long and tedious task of copying the original letters so they could be preserved and I could have working copies; my old friend Lucille Horne for always inquiring about my progress and keeping me motivated; J. Robert McNutt, M.D., for his interest and providing me with specific information; my friends Chuck and Jan Anderson for their kind and gentle perusal of my early manuscript; the Arnold Macdonald family for excellent suggestions; Vinnie and Helen Hinson, Bob and Eleanor Burnham, Harold Bly, Ray and Marilynn Goodale, Harold and Priscilla Chapman, and Ted Dillard for their encouragement; my sister-in-law, Barbara Lassen, for vital genealogical information and searching. Chris Catanese, whom I met through the Marco Island Civil War Club, has been a great help and motivator to bring this project to a close and put me in touch with knowledgeable folks in the publishing field. Bob Milbier has spent hours helping me edit and cheered me on when doubts crept in. My cousins, Margaret Faulks and Elizabeth Hanf, were enormously helpful in providing old family photos and contributing family remembrances. In Michigan, Tom Nanzig, of the Ann Arbor Civil War Round Table, generously gave of his time to critique my original manuscript and offer valuable suggestions. I am very grateful to Jean Burke, a local artist and friend, who gave me some wonderful ideas for artwork. A very special thank you to old friends, Deke and Polly Bardsley, for the kind use of their wonderful antique cottage by the sea. The inspiration I gained there was deeply personal and enabled me to put the finishing touches on my manuscript.

Technologically, I must thank two people: Mike DeMopoulos for scanning my original, typewritten manuscript onto a disk so I could do the rewriting on my computer, and John Maguire, who spent hours preparing the illustrations and printed up the final manuscript.

I am most grateful to O. B. Curtis, author of *History of the Twenty-fourth Michigan of the Iron Brigade*. He was a member of the regiment and was, I believe, responsible for the hand-drawn maps that appear in this book.

Most of all I want to thank my family: my husband, Bob Lassen, and my children, Pam and Rob. My parents, Robert and Harriet Peel, and my sister, Pat Trumpoldt, all three of whom are now deceased, would be so happy to know that I have finally "done something" with the letters. Thank you from the bottom of my heart.

I feel a deep gratitude for all the folks at Indiana University Press. Their understanding of my ignorance of the publishing process, their continuing courtesy of keeping me informed of the progress of my manuscript on its journey toward publication, and their wonderful expertise were all hugely appreciated.

Your friend, cousin, wife, mother, daughter, and sister,
Coralou Lassen

Introduction

These letters are especially poignant because young John Pardington was killed July 1, 1863, at the Battle of Gettysburg; he never again saw his wife, Sarah, or infant daughter, Maria, after bidding them farewell the previous summer. At John's request, Sarah saved his letters, and as the years went by, they became a way for his daughter to know him. John spoke from the heart, sometimes eloquently, yet his misspellings, poor punctuation, and occasional bad grammar have all been retained to present an honest rendering of his feelings, thoughts, and dreams. In some cases, however, I have added capital letters and periods at the ends of sentences to make it more comfortable for the reader. Now and then John adds a charming sketch at the beginning or end of a letter. In February of 1863, he composed a moving poem commemorating the six-month anniversary of his departure. The great appeal of the letters is the human touch, not the history of the Civil War or discussions of battle strategies.

John Henry Pardington and Sarah Ann Knapp, both in their early twenties, were married December 29, 1860, in the village of Trenton, Michigan. Their daughter, Maria, named after John's sister, was born June 11, 1862, just two and a half months before her father left for the battlefield. To support his family, John worked as a clerk in a local store.

In the early summer of 1862, President Lincoln issued an urgent call for more enlistments. Responding to this emergency, the mayor of Detroit called a war meeting for July 15. An announcement in the *Detroit Free Press* said:

> To Arms! The Union is now in its greatest peril. Unless the people rush to the flag, the days of American glory will be gone forever. Let the meeting be marked by harmony, enthusiasm, patriotism. Let every

man forget party and behold only his imperiled country. The federal union must be preserved. The folds of the flag must wave forever over all the territory the fathers left us or which we acquired by the blood and treasure of the nation.

Judge Henry A. Morrow, soon to become Colonel Morrow, spoke at the meeting:

Fellow Citizens—We are met here now in the second crisis of our country. There is a mistaken feeling that this meeting is preliminary to a draft. Enough can be procured without such measures. Everyone who can should go, and the men who stay at home must support the families of those who go. Those of us who have no families should go. I do propose that men of families shall perform duties that we young men should perform. Let each man ask himself: "Will I go?" I have already said I would. The government has done as much for me as for you and I am ready to assist in upholding it.

The meeting ended in a mob riot spurred by many Secessionists and Southern sympathizers, who had crossed the Detroit River from Canada where they had sought refuge. It was a sorry spectacle, and local citizens were deeply humiliated. In response to this indignity, concerned citizens met many nights and days thereafter, vowing to raise an extra regiment in addition to their quota. It seemed everyone was infected with patriotic fervor.

On August 6, 1862, John enlisted as a private in Capt. Isaac Ingersoll's Company B of the Twenty-fourth Michigan Volunteers. The regiment consisted of 1,030 men; they were an interesting mix of rich and poor, whose occupations and professions ranged from clerking and farming to medicine and law. The youngest was thirteen and the oldest seventy. They were assigned to the famous Iron Brigade, well known for its valor and courage.

On August 29, 1862, amid waving banners, bands playing, and a tremendous outpouring of patriotism, John said goodbye to his wife and daughter and left Detroit with the Twenty-fourth Michigan. One can only imagine the fullness of the moment. John described that leave-taking with deep feeling and colorful detail in his letter dated September 24, 1862.

The next several weeks found the men of the Twenty-fourth engaged in intense drilling and training. They were first tested in December at the Battle of Fredericksburg where their gallantry earned them new respect from the already seasoned soldiers of the Iron Brigade. After the Battle of Fredericksburg, they went into winter quarters near Belle Plaine,

Virginia, where, with the exception of a few forays, the months of January through April were spent fighting illness, drilling, and preparing for renewed fighting in late April and early May. The Battle of Chancellorsville, another Union defeat, brought heavy casualties but did not dampen their resolve to "crush the Rebellion."

As you read the June letters, you will begin to notice a change in John's attitude. He appears to be more aware of his mortality and the possibility that the war will last longer than originally anticipated. In his last letter, written June 22, 1863, he speaks of his loneliness and his yearning for home.

For more than one hundred and thirty-five years these letters have been treasured by my family. It now gives me great pleasure to share them with you.

Coralou Peel Lassen,
great-granddaughter of
John and Sarah Pardington

Explanation of Names

John Henry Pardington [*Jack*]

Husband of Sarah
Father of baby Maria
Corporal in the Twenty-fourth Michigan Volunteers, Company B

Sarah Ann Knapp Pardington

Wife of John
Mother of Maria

Baby Maria [*pronounced "Mariah"*]

Infant daughter of John and Sarah Pardington, named after his sister, Maria. Often referred to as "Baby."

Joseph and Belinda Van Horn

Sister and brother-in-law of Sarah
Witnesses at their wedding, December 29, 1860

Maria and Maryann

Sisters of John
Maria was Mrs. Richard H. Carter of Toledo, Ohio

Elias Knapp

Brother of Sarah
Member of Eighteenth New York Regiment

dear Sarah

Jim McIlhiny

Close friend and soldier in Twenty-fourth Michigan, Company B

Bob McDonald

Robert McDonald, mentioned in the first letter, became Sarah's second husband

Father

Sarah's father, Benjamin Fairchild Knapp, who was also father of Elias and nine other children

George McDonald

Brother of Robert McDonald, became Sarah's third husband after Robert died

dear Sarah

Prologue

In the summer of 1862, John Pardington writes to Mary, his sister-in-law, announcing the birth of his daughter, Maria. The young clerk and his wife, Sarah, have moved recently to a new, larger house, set in a grove of fruit trees, in the small Michigan village of Trenton on the Detroit River. Mother and daughter are doing well, he writes, and though he longs for a job "out-doors," he makes a good living "clearking." They are happy and comfortable, John tells Mary, "and I hope we always will be so."

When Mary next hears from them, all of their lives have abruptly changed.

Trenton
June 18/62

Mary Dear Sister[1]

It is with Pleasure I take up my Pen to inform you that Sarah has been sick and doing well and she has got a little daughter.[2] It is a week old to day and is smart as a cricket and is well. Dear Sister I have moved from where I lived when Marcia[3] left. I have moved across the road in a larger house and about forty bearing frouit trees Peach Plum and apples. I Pay fifty dollars a year for the house. It is a nice one a good seller and a good accomodation in every way. Dear Sister I am so glad Sarah is getting so smart and well and so is the baby. We are liveing Happy and comfortably and I hope we always will be so. I am making a good living clearking but it dont agree with me very well. I have no appetite. If I could get any thing to do out-doors to Pay me as well I would quit but if I cant why I shall stay at it this summer and winter God willing. Say Mary I should like to see you firstrate. I have seen them all But you. But never mind I shall see you after awhile I hope. Dear Sister I have not much more to say at Present. The custemers are a waiting to be served. I must say good By. I will write you a longer [letter] the next time. Answer this when you get it. Sarah and me unite in love to all and of course the *Babys*.

I remain Yours Truly
John H. Pardington
Trenton

1. Mary Knapp Noble, sister of Sarah and wife of David Noble, who, soon after this letter was written, was killed in the war.

2. Maria Pardington, daughter of John and Sarah Pardington, born June 11, 1862.

3. Another sister of Sarah.

Trenton
August 17/62

Dear Sister Mary

I will try after a long time to write to you. I am in trouble Mary for John is going to the war. He leaves Detroit in about two weeks. O Mary what a cruel war this is. May we all mourn your great loss, little did I think we would be called to mourn Daveds [loss] so soon.

John is going and God only knows how soon I may be called to mourn like you but I will try and hope for the best. If I had no baby I would go with him. O Mary I have got a sweet little girl. How I wish you could see her. I wish you could come home this fall. It must be so lonesom and we all want to see you so bad to. How are the children, Marcia and her children. Henry McDonald has enlisted in the same company with John. Ira fletcher has inlisted in the same regiment but not in the same company. Morrows 24th Regiment is the one our boys are a going in. A new Regiment and called the best regiment in the State.

Sep the 14 1862

Well Sister it has been a gret while since I comenced this. Sow will try and finish it. I have moved down to Jos[1] again. John is gone and is now in Alexandria. I had a letter from him last week. He was well and in good spirits. O how lonely I am since he went away. My baby is such lots of company to me now. O how I do want to see you. I beleive we could be great company to one a nother. Jos folks are all well. Belinda has comensed a letter to one of you girls and I dont know but boath. Dear Sister when I get to thinking it nearly drives me crazy. I dont dare to think any more than I can help. O Mary I have got a sweet baby and she is a great comfort to me and I hope she will all ways prove a comfort to her Mother. O it is so hard to part with our Husbands in this way. If we could be with them in theyr sickness and know that they wer well taken care of we could be more reconedsiled to our lot. O it makes my hart ake to think. Mary I hope you will answer this leter soon. I wont have so much to do but what I can write sooner next time. Give my love to Marcia and children and tell them to write. Tell the children that Aunt Sarah wants to see them all very much. Tell wilber that he must be a very good boy to his Mother and help her all he can and his Aunt Sarah and every body else will love him and think a great deal of him. I will tell you where to direct to John if you will write to him.

> John H. Pardington
> Co. B 24 Michigan Regiment
> Washington D.C.

We have not heard from Elias[2] yet. John said he would find out about him if he could.

Write soon

> This from your sister
> Sarah A Pardington

1. Joseph and Belinda Van Horn, sister and brother-in-law of Sarah.
2. Elias Knapp was a brother of Sarah, Mary, Marcia, and Belinda.

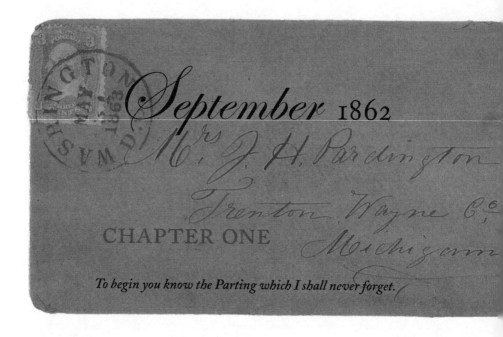

September 1862

CHAPTER ONE

To begin you know the Parting which I shall never forget.

We can only imagine the many different emotions felt by the men that first night in camp. Many had never been away from home before. They were lonely, confused, and frightened, wondering how the folks at home were coping with their absence. Sons worried about their parents, husbands and fathers about their wives and children. The raw recruits wondered if they would be brave in battle. Would they even know how to fight? So far, they were relatively untrained, and the realities of war were unknown and probably somewhat romanticized.

Their send-off on August 29 was heroic. In his book *The Twenty-fourth Michigan,* Donald L. Smith described the exciting scene:

> Cheering and singing had started as the Regiment was forming. Woodward Avenue was pulsing with an unexampled intensity. For hours people had swarmed upon every standing place along the route. The National colors were everywhere, making a carnival scene. They were draped across the streets, hung from windows, carried by children, as the populace prepared to send the Regiment off. It was less a march than a triumphal procession. As one corporal put it, "Roman emperor never had a prouder greeting." Street, sidewalk, windows, roofs, balconies, anywhere that people could hang, stand, or sit, were jammed with spectators. As soon as the people at any point caught sight of the long blue line and saw the shimmer of the bayonets, they took up a cheering that never ceased. Handkerchiefs fluttered in the

air like butterflies. Eyes, many of them dim with tears and wet with pride, gazed upon the ranks as they passed. Through an avenue literally jammed, giving way before them and closing in dense masses behind, the companies marched.

They traveled by steamer to Cleveland. It was a stormy trip, so all were grateful to board a train for the journey to Pittsburgh. Townsfolk all along the way gathered to cheer them as they passed by. In Pittsburgh, the *Gazette* reported, "The Twenty-fourth Michigan arrived in this city Saturday evening, August 30. Its soldiers are of the very best class of men, stout, hearty, cheerful, intelligent, and splendidly equipped. They were marched to the city hall, where a sumptuous repast awaited them, during which Colonel Morrow [commander of the Twenty-fourth Michigan] made a patriotic address."

Reality set in on September 1 with their arrival in Washington. The journey had been long, tiring, and delayed many times when they were sidetracked for passing trains. Torrential rains battered them as they marched down Pennsylvania Avenue on their way to Alexandria. Passing them by were ambulances carrying the wounded from nearby battlefields.

At home, Sarah, missing her husband terribly, found solace in tending to her infant daughter, Maria, and writing to her sister, Mary Noble, who had recently lost her husband, David, to the war. Sarah and the baby eventually went to live with another sister, Belinda, and her husband, Joseph Van Horn.

The month of September found the Twenty-fourth Michigan moving to various camps, drilling, becoming more skilled with weaponry, and, in general, toughening up. Their preparation for joining the famous Iron Brigade was serious business indeed. On September 29, the regiment received orders to join the Army of the Potomac led by General McClellan in Frederick, Maryland. Once again they traveled by rail through beautiful countryside, passing by the old flag being displayed at simple cottages and grand estates alike. Most folks along the route called out their greetings and waved. An occasional few stood quietly and watched them pass without a gesture. They arrived in the Monocacy Valley, found a good campsite, and settled into a routine of more drilling and cleaning of clothes. When they had time off, a few fished in the river. Being tested in battle was still a challenge to be faced in the unknown future, and John's letters indicated an eagerness to be done with it and return home. Little did they know what lay ahead.

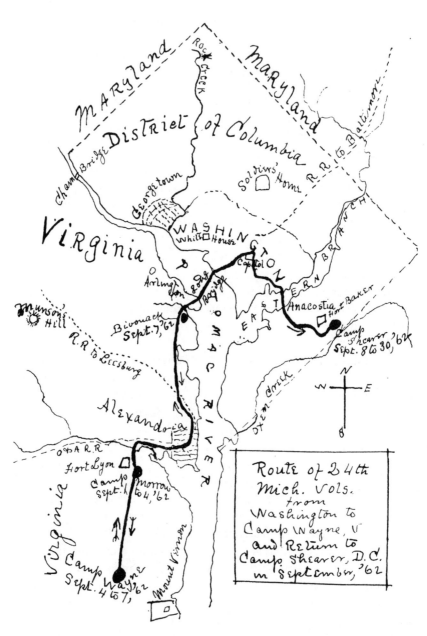

Route of Twenty-fourth Michigan Volunteers from Washington to Camp Wayne, Virginia, and Return to Camp Shearer, D.C., in September 1862

Fort Lyons Alexandria
September 2, 1862

Dear Wife,

It is in Haste I write these few lines to you for we are now under marching orders either to Bull Run or back to Washington. The enemys cavalry are now in full force a few miles from us. We have not a round of ammunition with us although in enemy country. There was five men shot on Picket only a little ways from us last night. They are having awful work here. They Put us through from Washington yesterday on a force march here with our heavy loads on our back. Hundreds drop out of Rank with fatague. Dear we are all in good spirits and well. We arrived here last night and just as we got here it comes on a heavy rain storm. Not a tent to cover us but I soon found out a old shed just about like Joes old cow shed and I slept good till morning although wet through. They have Put us through a little to heavey since we started. Night and day and here we are on the sacred soil of Old verginia. I am on gaurd to day and to night. My time will be off tomorrow at nine Oclock. I will write again directly we get settled. Dear Sarah the ambulences is one Perfect string of wounded going into Washington. I see Bob McDonald[1] in Baltimore. He is getting along first Rate. Dear Sarah I dont think it will be long before we are ordered to the Battle feild. If it aint today some thinks that is our Plase of Destination. Hope not yet on the mens account for we are not drilled yet good enough. But if that should be the case not a man will flinch. Dear Wife kiss the Baby for me and keep up good spirits for hers and mines accounts. Today is as cool as any I have seen in Michigan. Dear Sarah dont write till you hear from me again for I dont know where we will be stationed. Remember me to all enquireing friends Jo and Belinda and Willie[2] and Mr Clee. Tell them I will write when I can get time. Excuse this for it was wrote on the ground. Kiss the Baby and except one for yourself. Good By good By God Bless you.

I remain your affec Husband
John H. Pardington
Co. B Cap Ingersall
24 Michigan Infantry

P.S. Dont write till I write again. Kiss Mother for me.

Jack

1. Robert McDonald, Fourth Michigan, Company I, became Sarah's second husband on October 23, 1864.
2. William Sanders, a very close friend of John's and Sarah's.

dear Sarah

My Dear Wife

You will think it strange when you receive another letter from me But I will tell you the reason why. We have different orders. We are going to stay where we are for the Present for we expect a great battle here in a few days. Our army is faling back to Alexandria and the Rebels are in full foarce behind so you may expect to hear something from the 24th Reigment in a few days. We are all supplied with Plenty of ammunition and we sleep on our arms at night. The enemy aint over ten miles from us. Dear Sarah the 18th New York[1] will be with us in a few days. I will find out Elias and then write to you about him. There will be a great Battle here in a few days which I think will Decide the events of the war. It is the Rebels last chance and they fight like Devils. Dear Sarah there was a whole Bragade came in today and they were numbered no more than our reigment. Our troops have hard work but are in good spirits and Bound to Whip them. Dear Sarah when you direct your letters Write them

John H Pardington
Co. B 24th Michigan Regiment
Washington D.C.

P.S. Dear Wife Kiss the Baby for me and Write as soon as you get this and tell me the news at home for when I write again I suppose I shall tell you if I am spared how being on a battle feels. Remember me to all and a Kiss for the Baby and except one for yourself. So good By God Bless you give me your Prayers. Kiss Mother for me and remember me to Buttons[2] folk and all in Trenton. If you see them mind Willie and Mr Clee and God Bless you and a Kiss. So good By I remain your affec Husband

John H Pardington
Co. B Cap Ingersal 24th Mich Infantry
Washington D.C.

Sarah When you Write send me a stamp with it if you please.

Jack

Dear Sarah our Regiment is made the advance of the Army of the Potomic and our Company is Detached for Skirmshers so you know how they Put Michigan men through.

John

1. The Eighteenth New York Regiment was the unit with which Elias Knapp, Sarah's brother, served.

2. Probably Augustus Button, a cooper from Trenton, Michigan, and father of Edward Button, a friend of John's.

Sunday Sep 14, 1862
Camp Shearer
Fort Baker
Washington D.C.

Dearest Wife

Last night I received your kind and affec letter and was glad to hear from my little wife and my baby. O Sarah you cant think how eager I tore open the envelope to read the preacious line which thrilled through me and made my heart light and Happy. O Sarah you cant think how that few lines Put me in such good spirits. Dear Sarah do write me a long letter the next time not as I grumble at the one you wrote me no indeed far from [it]. Dear Sarah we have moved from the plase when I wrote my first letter. We have moved about 3 miles from Washington on the line of defences around the city. We are right by Fort Baker. Dear Sarah about sleeping and eating you never heard of a soldier getting the best. We fare Pretty well but the marches is what uses the soldier up the most. Dear Sarah we can now hear heavay firing in the distance suppose to be between the armies of McClellen and the Rebel Jackson. They must be fighting hard by the constant and hevey fireing. Dear I am going to Prayer meeting to night with James Havens[1] in the Chaplin tent. We have a good many church members in the 24th. Dear Sarah it [is] now getting dark and I must now soon close my letter. But first tell me about what you done with your money and about your Order, Sarah excuse me for mentinont them. But you know Sarah it is my duty. Forgive me dear if I have done any harm for I ment none. Kiss mother for me and Remember Her to me My Dear. Kiss Belinda[2] for me But dont tell Jo. or let him see you do it. Now Kiss the Baby for Little Dear How I would like to see her the dear little thing.

Good By God Bless you is my Prayer. Remember me to all and except a Kiss from your loveing Husband

J H Pardington
Co. B 24th Mich Infantry
Washington D.C.

P.S. Sarah send a dollar or two I Bought a revolver and it used up my money. Mind the stamp.

Good By god Bless you

John

dear Sarah

a Kiss

Write soon

1. One of the "Trenton Boys" in Company B.
2. Sarah's sister. Sarah and Baby Maria went to live with Belinda and her husband when John left for the war.

Sunday
Camp Shearer Fort Baker
Sep 21
Washington D.C.

My Dear Wife

I received your kind and affectinate [letter] Last night and was glad to hear from you and baby. I Suppose you have received my letter By this time for I wrote it the day you wrote yours on the 14th day Sep. Dear Sarah be careful of little maria for you say the scarlet fever is very bad around trenton. Sarah if Jos children get it move up to mothers' and stay awhile. Not move your things but just yourself for I would not lose that little one for anything. It would make me reckless and I hope the lord willing she will be spared to us and excapes those dangerous fevers. Dear Sarah I took very sick yesterday but I am getting a little better today. I was took with a Pain in my chest and I went to the hospatel for some mediceni and they gave me a dose of stuf which I thought would kill me. Thats what ail me now. I dont beleive they know what they was giveing me. They gave me a dose of Rhubarb. Why it was a teaspoonful besides something else in it all at one dose, and I was never better in my life before only that pain in my chest. What makes me sick is the cause of the stuff they gave me. They dont care some how or other but I was pretty sick last night. God forbid that i shall be any worse for Dear Sarah you have no Idea of what sickness is here. Give me the chance of the Bullets than the Hospetal.

Dear Sarah you say you was lonesom. What do you think of me away from friends and *one* that is so near and dear to me? You have got friends around you. But dear I hope the day will not be far distant when we shall clasp each others neck and Print a warm kiss of love on each other lips. Keep up spirits dear for my sake and that dear little Angel. Sarah have you heard from Maria?[1] If you have I wish you would write and tell me and tell Maryann[2] to write to me. Tell me all the news. Dear Sarah I had my hair cut all off short so I send you a lock of it which I know you will except it. I did not Plaid it. You wont care though will you dear. I wish you would Plaid some of yours and send it to me in your next [letter] and I will give you a good kiss when I come home. Remember me to all at home and all joes folks and the rest around there. Sarah I will send you my picture when I receive another letter from [you] for I want a little money from you. Excuse me for naming it but then I bought a revolver wich took all of it so you will not mind will you dear. Sarah you can all talk about volentering but if [I] was at home I think I should stay there for I know now how to appreciate your company and if ever I come [home] the Lord Willing I think I shall not give you any cause again to set up for me nights like you used to. Sarah if I could recall those nights I would sacriface my right hand But you will forgive me wont you dear and I make a faithful Promise before God if ever I get back to you I will live a different life.

Sarah I am trying to live a different one here and I hope the Lord Helping me I shall return a Christian. Pray for me Sarah that I may. We have nice Prayer meetings and class meeting and good Preaching Sunday which is a good Benefit to us. I am shure we ought to be thankful for. Ira is well. Raynors[3] wife's brother is well. He is a nice young fellow and a member of the church. If you see Maria tell her I seen her old Beau Ed Sackrider. He is Post master in the 17th Mich Reigment. He is well. I have not seen Elias yet. We are farther off him now. I think it will be a Poor chance to see him now. Good By god Bless you and little maria and both of you except a loveing kiss from your loveing Husband John H Pardington

Co. B 24th Michigan Infantry
Washington D.C.

Write soon never mind Paper ink and stamp as long as you have got money *and Health*

Jack

1. John's sister Maria.
2. John's sister Maryann.
3. Reverend Rayner Stevens Pardington, John's brother, who was married to Eliza Cory, sister of Reuben Cory, who was also a member of the Twenty-fourth Michigan in Company D.

Wednesday Sep 24 1862 Camp Schearer D.C.

Dear Wife,

Haveing a little spare time to spare I thought I would write you a few lines Incident to our jurney which I never mentioned in my letter. To begin you know the Parting which I shall never forget the last kiss. We arrived at Cleveland after a rather rough Passage about 8 Oclock PM. We staid at the depoe about one or two hours and then started for Pittsburgh. I shall never forget that Plase as long as I live. The Pepole was so Patriote [patriotic]. They gave us a first[rate] supper in their best Hall in the city, and then we got aboard [one] of the cars which runs in the center of the streets. We staid there about 2 hours in the cars Both sides being lined with Ladies and young girls and men. The girls would climb up to the windows and give us their Handkercheifs to remember [them] by I got six. Excuse me Sarah. But I did not take for that. But because I thought they would be useful to me. So you will forgive me wont you. I know you will. The next Plase we started for was Baltimore. We arrived there on sunday afternoon about 4 oclock. We marched down to the depot and got Plenty to eat, But had to slep on the sidewalk all night wich I though[t] rather hard after being used to a good feather Bed and a good Bedfellow. We had no covering only our Blankets and wet to the ground. That was all very well so far But the worst is to come yet. The next morning we started for washington. We arrived about 10 oclock A.M. We had Lunch there and started for fort Lyons about 3 miles beyond Alexandria where the Brave Ellsworth[1] fell so nobly. Mind you we had our heavy knapscacks on our Back, under a Burning sun in all about 15 miles. We arrived there about sundown and just as we got there it set in a terrible thunder Storm and rained tremendious. We had no tents nor nothing to eat. Our tents and Provisions had not come up. We had nothing to do but dump down on the ground almost up to anlkes in water. But Jack thought that would not do for him. So off I started and some more [men] to an old Secesh House.[2] We offered the Old Devil a dollar apeice to sleep on the cellar floor But he would not do it. But we was Bound not to be outdone. So off we started for the Barn but that was locked. We dare not break it in. It was raining awful hard all the time. Wet to the skin and cold. No supper either so we had to be satisfied with the old cow shed shit and all. Was not that Pleasent Sarah. I think it was. I slept first rate. But when I awoke in the morning I could hardly move so stiff and sore But in good spirits for the morning Broke in splendour and we soon got warm beneath the warmth and splender of a southern sun. We are encamped in a better situation now. Good and Plenty to eat and good Place to sleep. But we cant tell how long we may stay. We may [stay] all the winter and we may not stay a day. All according whaether they need us or not. Cant tell the fortunes of war. They are drilling us right through now and they are not doing it for nothing I can tell you. The Rebels lost 20 thousand in their Battles in Maryland[3] and they have retreted from that state and not one left. They did not make much. Tell

Jo McClellan is the man for to do the Busines. He is following them right up and now is the time for Richmond and an end to the Rebelion and Death to all Traitors is the War cry. Dear Sarah I must soon End with my kind Love to all And except the same from your Loveing Husband.

John H. Pardington
Co. B 24 Michigan Infantry
Washington D.C.

Kiss little Maria for me. How I would like to see her. When I think of her and you dear it often brings tears into my eyes wich I cannot stop. I let them come for it releives me much. Except a sweet Kiss.

P.S. Write soon and Write often. I have not received any answer from you But except [expect] one to night. I look forward for the time very anxious I tell you. Remember to all Jos folks.

Forward on "W" march Gaurd

1. According to the May 25, 1861, edition of the *Philadelphia Inquirer,* Colonel E. E. Ellsworth, a highly esteemed man who served, at Lincoln's special request, as a member of the president's personal escort, was assassinated by a secessionist. This occurred when Colonel Ellsworth went to the roof of an Alexandria hotel and removed a Rebel flag, replacing it with the Stars and Stripes. On returning from the roof, he was confronted by a Rebel sympathizer who shot him, killing him almost instantly. It was said that President Lincoln was "greatly afflicted" by Colonel Ellsworth's death.

2. This refers to houses occupied by secessionists or southern sympathizers.

3. The Battle of Antietam.

dear Sarah

My Dear Wife

I receved your kind and affec letter Friday Dated Late Saturday night Sep 20 1862. Dear Sarah you must not set up too late on account of your health. I was glad to hear from you and Oh that I could receive a letter every day, for Sarah you dont know how it helps to keep up my spirits to hear from you and baby. In regard to my health I suppose you have received my other letters. I was pretty sick but I am well now only when I get up mornings I have awful pains in my Back and sides which however soon goes off when I move around. But they bother me a good deal I think it is from sleeping so much on the ground. But I oppose [suppose] I soon have to get used to that. I wrote you a letter the other day about our jurney from Detroit. Tell me in your next if you have received it will you dear. I shall Write and Post a letter for Father When I send this. Dear Sarah about that money. You know what I said in detroit before I left. You Know Father wanted $50 and I told him that your Father wanted it and I had refused him and therefore I could not let him have any. Then it could be showing no partiaality, and I think your father did not right in asking you for it for he knowed very well that you would not refuse him. But dear Sarah let that drop. We are having good times here now. We have a sham fight here every day. We have ten to twenty rounds of Blank cartridge gave us and we march off about half a mile. There we go through the form of Battle about 400 on a side. Each side has a flag the colelon [colonel] on one side and the major on the other. I think myself it is a bad Practice for there is always three or four get wounded or hurt for they get so excited they dont know what they are doing. One man yesterday afternoon fired his ramrod a steel one at that. It struck a man right on the knee But it struck him lengthways so it did hurt very bad. But he had to be carried in a waggon in to camp. We general[ly] fire within about 4 or 5 rods of one another so you see if they put in anything in thire gun it is going to hit somebody. The first day we had a sham fight some man put in a ball. It struck a man on our left just a little ways from me. The ball passed through his pants right by the thigh and made quite a flesh wound. If it had struck him one inch further it would have Broke his leg all to peices so you can see there is some hard kases in the Reigment. The second day four got wounded. One had his eyes almost shot out and another had his fingers shot half off. But it is fun after all taken one another Prisoners. The next time I am going to make a dash for one of the Captains. I will get him to if I can get some good Backers. But Enough of that so I will say good By to fighting. Sarah you asked me about going down to Marias when she went back. Suit yourself only I would like to have my letters answers as quick as possible for they are the only thing that keeps up my spirits now. But Sarah act according to your own concience and that will Suit me, for you dont know when a letter will come very urgent and if you should be away and not get it till it was to late what would you think and how would you feel? But Sarah Please yourself if you want to go Sarah I do not want to put any restraint on your happiness or enjoying yourself. Give my love to Allie Button, Mary Ann and all the rest of the family. Give them my address so they can write to me. Give my love to Mother and tell her I am very sorry that she has had such a Bad fall. Tell her she will soon here from me. Now dear Sarah I dont want you to think that this is a cool letter because I love [you] just the same as Ever and a little Better for now I know How to appreciate your company when I get home God willing. Sarah I dont think it will be long before we are in active service in the fields. We are getting well drilled and in fighting order. I have not much more to say but give love to all and Jo folks and kiss the Baby for me and except one sweet one from your loveing Husband

John H. Pardington
Co. B 24 Mich. Infantry. Washington D.C.

Write as soon as you get this.

P.S. Sarah I will send you my Picture in my next [letter]. I had not time to get it this time. I am much Obliged to you for that which you sent me and in return I will send you a kiss on this leaf of Clover.

Yours forever
John

In Haste
Monday 29, 1862
Camp Shearer D.C.

Dearest Wife

I wrote you a letter yesterday and Hasten to write you a few lines, we have received marching order this morning, to hasten to Gen. McClellen. We start to morrow at 9 o clock or this evening. We go By railroad to Frederick and thence to the grand army of the Patomic. So Sarah farwell for the Present. You will no doubt hear from the 24th in good time. They want to Bring in a foarce enough to crush the Rebellnon. Good By God Bless and Protect you. Give my love to all and Kiss the dear little Maria. In good spirits Your Loving Husband

J. H. Pardington

dear Sarah

In Haste For we are Packing up
Dear Sarah Direct your letters
    J. H. Pardington
    Frederick, Maryland
    Co. B 24th Mich. Infantry
    Gen. McClellan Army

Tell them all so that want to write

                                                John

A Kiss

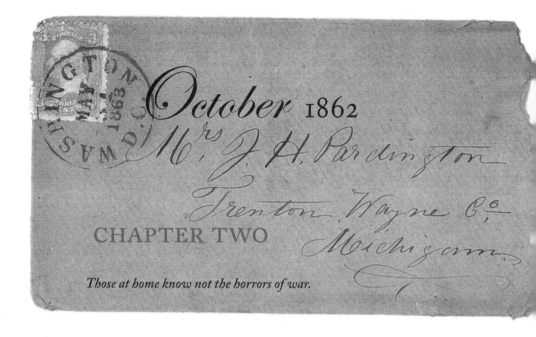

October 1862

16ᵗʰ J. H. Pardington

Trenton, Wayne Co,

Michigan

CHAPTER TWO

Those at home know not the horrors of war.

October brought exhaustion and humiliation to the Twenty-fourth Michigan Volunteers. Battle-toughened remnants of the Iron Brigade, veterans of the massacre at Antietam, wrongfully believed that the fresh recruits of the Twenty-fourth were "bounty men" and greeted them with derision and hostility. Bounty men were paid well by the state to enlist, so men who had voluntarily left their homes and loved ones considered it insulting to accept a bounty.

Donald L. Smith described the welcome this way:

> As the Twenty-fourth Michigan marched onto the parade ground, across from them they saw the mighty Iron Brigade, consisting of the Nineteenth Indiana, Second, Sixth, and Seventh Wisconsin Volunteers, standing with the natural ease of the battle-hardened infantryman. They were lean, hard, and sunburned men, with the look and attitude of those who had stared death in the face on more than one occasion and not been found wanting. They were wearing their famous black hats, the badge of honor the Brigade was permitted to wear, instead of the forage caps common to the rest of the army. Coldness and hostility was in their glance and in their bearing. These were veterans, men who had proved themselves in combat, not recruits and upstarts who aspire to recognition as such. If the Twenty-fourth wanted to join these men, they would have to earn the right; it would not be given to them.

Before this sad spectacle occurred, the regiment had been in high spirits. October 4 was a banner day! The Twenty-fourth Michigan, in formation and filled with great excitement, honored their leader and hero, Abraham Lincoln, as the president's train passed slowly by while he reviewed the troops. John was deeply moved to see him. It was customary for the troops to deride or complain about politicians, but the president was an exception. Most of the men revered him.

Even though the Twenty-fourth moved frequently during the month, drilling intensely at each camp, the mail caught up with them. Sarah's letters arrived a week to ten days after she sent them. John was "much pleased" to receive the lock of hair she sent and asked her for a picture of the baby, as he already had a "likeness" of her safely tucked away in his watch pocket. He also asked Sarah to send a dollar or two so he could purchase some much-needed food. John was intrigued by the coincidence of President Lincoln's Emancipation Proclamation becoming law on January 1, 1863, John's twenty-fourth birthday.

A great sense of urgency engulfed the troops toward the end of October; they felt a battle was imminent. With the exception of the many men who had fallen ill in the Brigade, they were ready for it. The Iron Brigade was on the march again, passing the recent battlefield of Antietam and crossing South Mountain. General Gibbon remarked after reviewing the Twenty-fourth Michigan again, "This regiment is the best drilled, after such a short term of service, of any I have ever reviewed." Colonel Morrow's efforts had paid off. He was determined to win for the regiment the respect of the Iron Brigade.

Sunday Oct. 5 1862
Frederick Maryland

Dear Wife

Not feeling well enough to go to meeting to day I thought I would sit down and write to the loved one at home. For I feel quite miserable this morning that I can hardly write. So you will excuse dear Sarah all mistakes and scribling. We went down to the Nicromancy River[1] yesterday and washed all our clothes, and that is only what we have on our Back so we had to sit naked for about 2 or 3 hours in the sun till our things dried. I think that['s] what makes me sick today we were called away from our

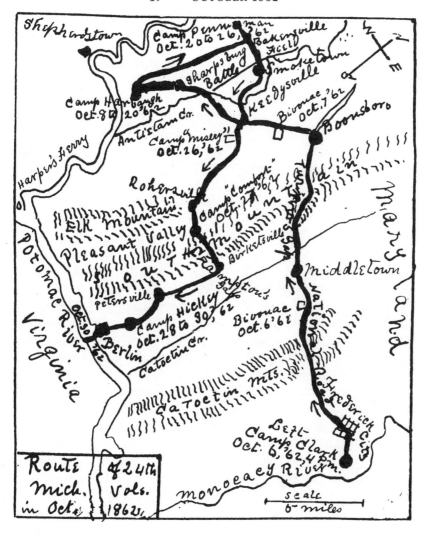

Route of Twenty-fourth Michigan Volunteers in October 1862

old camp ground in such a hurry that we had to leave everything behind even my housewife[2] and everything. We have not even a change of clothes with us and I do not think we will ever see them again till after the war. Dear Sarah I saw Old Father Abe Lincoln yesterday. He passed through here. He has been visiting the Army of the Potomic. Dear Sarah when you see his picture you see him. He is a very tall man and looks very old and careworn. He Bowed very Politely to us. Seward[3] was with him. Sarah the north is getting an awful foarce in here and Harperferry. We expect to leave here every moment for we are under Marching Orders now for sharpsburg so you see dear Sarah we do not stay long now in a Plase. They expect Hot work here in a few days. We will have to be in it. They that is the north is getting such a force in here against the Rebels that I hope the next Battle will be the Decisive one. Dear Sarah those at home know not the horrors of war. We do not know much But what I have seen [h]as gave me a Pretty good insight to it. To see the Poor wounded at Washington some without arms and legs Some no hand some no finger. I see one Poor fellow a Peace of shell struck him on the right hand took off one of his fingers then struck his left hand tore his hand and arm and split it almost to his shoulder. Passed on and killed and wounded 5 or six others. Mind you just one fragment of shell or one Peice and that is nothing to the numerous incidents. What an awful sight of cripples there will be after this war. Dear Sarah this war cant last much longer at this rate. Dear Sarah Frederick is quite a nice city that is the Plase where Jackson[4] met such a Poor reception and McClellen[5] met such a good one. It [is] a splendid country. I should like to live here after the war it is so hilly and wattered so well with running streams. Dear Sarah we are now under Gen Hooker.[6] "Fighting Jo" rather thats what he is named. I think we will start tomorrow. If not we will not be longer than Wednesday at any rate. When that Battle does come off you will no doubt hear of it in the Paper, but if we are in it and God spares my life or if I am only wounded if I can I will write soon as possible and let you know. The health of the 24th Reg is firstrate so far and all in good. Last Sunday I saw Nick Kettle. He looks kind of Hard I tell you after his usage by the Rebels. But his health is very good considering how he has fared. Sarah Love I have got your likeness safe yet. It was a good job I got this locket to keep it in for some of the other Boys have quite a truble to cary theirs for they are in cases. You see I can put mine in my watch pocket and have it with me all the time. It is just as plain as when I left. It is my only comfort now. When I gase on it and kiss it I can hardly stop the tears that would crowd into my eyes. Oh Sarah [no one] knows the sacrifice a man makes when he leaves Wife and child. If I had known it I think I should hardly had left But keep this to yourself. For I would not discourage any one for [en]listing for I think it is every man['s] duty. But if I was single it would be different. I think a single man ought not to stop a minute to think but start rightoff to shoulder his gun. A single man wont be thought much of in the north by the soldiers if he stayed at home when his Brave fellows are endureing all the hardships man can stand and they stay at home and quitely [quietly] look on. Shame on them for cowards. Dont you say so Sarah? I verily beleive the young girls would turn out enmass and help crush this terrible Rebellion. I know you would for one Sarah. Sarah give my love to all at home. Tell Jo I will write to him just as soon as I get time for we are so Busy at drilling we are getting quite efficient in the use of arms and I think when the 24th does get in action they will show them the way like the Brave 17th did. But enough Dear Sarah for I am going down in the city this afternoon to the Rebels sick down there and wounded for they had a fight before we come close to the city. Good By God Bless you and Baby. Bless the dear little one. Bring her up in the way of the Lord Dear Sarah. Pray to the Lord to help you love. A Kiss for Both of you. I remain your loveing Husband and Protector

> John H. Pardington
> Frederick Maryland
> Co. B 24th Michigan Infantry
> Gen McClellan Army

Write soon dear for they cheer me. This awful warm days but cold night[s]. I miss you dear Sarah.

Monday Morning

P.S. We are off tomorrow for Sharpsburgh. God Bless you.

> Jack

1. The Monocacy River.
2. A sort of backpack with essential personal items in it.
3. William H. Seward, secretary of state under President Lincoln.
4. General Thomas J. "Stonewall" Jackson, a Confederate general.
5. Union general George B. McClellan.
6. General Joseph Hooker, nicknamed "Fighting Joe."

Death to the Rebels no quarter is my cry

dear Sarah

Camp Harbaugh
Near Sharpsburgh Maryland
Friday Oct 10 1862

I have just received two letters from you one dated Sep 19, and one Oct 3 and O my dear you cant think what Pleasure and Emotion it gave me in Persuing these Prescious lines. Dear Sarah you little think where we are. We are where that last great Battle was fought. We have moved from w[h]ere we was. We are with the grand army of the Patomic. We are on this side of the Patomic. We are within a half of mile of the enemy Pickets. We can see them. They were shelling here yesterday driving the Rebels Back from the river. They make a awful noise when they Burst. Dear Sarah what an awful sight around here. You can see here and there little mounds denotes the resting Plase of many a gallant soldiers. Another Plase arms and legs drying in the sun, belongs to the Rebels. We have about one Hundred Rebels Wounded. The awfulest sight you ever see Sarah. Some Dying some legs off and arms and they are as lousey as they can be. They are lying in Barns and sheds just as they can get shelter. You ought to have Pass the Battle feild. We have Pass two now. On our last march we Passed the Battle feild of South Mountain where the Brave 17th made such a charge. There is about 200 dead Rebels Laying in the sun not Buried. I tell you dear Wife, we are just beginning to see service, there will be an awful Battle here in a few days and we will be in it of course for We are in Gen Hookers Corps. He goes by the name of fighting jo. Dear Wife I was sorry to hear of Mothers illness. I hope when you get this she will be Better tell Father I wrote to him. Has he Received [it]? Stay to Mothers as long as you can dear Sarah it is the Plase I would like to have you. I am so happy dear Sarah to hear you and the Baby (god Bless you Both) were so well. God grant that you may always be so But dear Sarah we have nothing to say. We must leave ourselves in his care. Dear Sarah I was much Pleased to you for your hair and I send you a Kiss for it. Kiss the Baby for me for hers. God Bless her. Dear Sarah how I long to see you Both. I would give all I am worth To be with you to night. But that cant be so we must hope for the Best. Dear Sarah you said about sending me a little money. Sometimes I wish you would send me a dollar or two now and then. For I need [it] sometimes. For when we get on a march we often get out of something to eat. And then a few Pennys come handy. Dear I have just Received a letter from Mary. She is well and wants my Picture but I cant send it. I will [send] you mine when I can get a chance to have it taken. I would like the Babys and yours first rate. But send the Babys any way. I have got yours yet and I keep it first rate in my watch Pocket. Dear Sarah I cant write any more at Present for this all the paper I could get. It is awful scarce here. But directly I can get some more Paper I will write a nother. Good By. God Bless you Both. Tell Mother I will write to her when I get some Paper. Kiss her for me and Remember me to all. We will Have some startling time here Pretty soon now.

Direct your letter John H. Pardington
Co. B 24th Mich Infantry
1st Army Corps
Gibbons Brigade
Washington D.C.

Your Ever True
and Loving Husband J. H. Pardington

Sunday Oct. 12/62
Camp Harbaugh
Sharpburgh, M.D.

My dear Wife

Since I wrote you those two letters We have received marching orders. Our cooks were called up last night at 12 o clock to cook two days raitions so we may be off at moments notice. There is four Brigades going. We do not know Where our Destination is But I tell you Sarah there will be Hot times here Pretty soon. Now we have heard that the Rebels envaded Pensyllvinas again. We thought at first we would go there But then we cant tell till we start. Before this letter reaches you we may be forty or fifty miles from there. We had a good meeting here to day. A good many of the soldiers attend meeting here. It is very Pleasent here. But getting rather cool, nights. Ira is well. He was over to our company last night and staid about one hour. Dear Sarah I have not much more to say in this note—for I wrote you all the news in the other letters. So good By. God Bless Both my little Dears. Enclose in this I send a note to mother. Give it to her without fails.

I remain Your Ever Faithful Husband
J H Pardington
Co. B 24 Mich Infantry
1st Army Corp
Gen. Gibbons Brigade
Washington D.C.

In Haste
Write soon
without fail

dear Sarah

My dear Wife

Seeing that I had a nother sheet of Paper and Borrowed some ink I thought I would write you a few more lines. It will seem strange tow letters coming together But I love to write to you. Better than Ever I did. I am almost ashamed to tell you but I dont care about writing to any body else. I have not wrote to any body else But you since I have been here. Only to Willie and Brother Bill and Mr Clee[1] one and Father one. I love to write to you. I could set all day and write to you if I had time. But we have not so I will write as often as I can and you will be satisfied wont you dear. My thoughts are about you and Baby all the time. O that I could see you both to morrow and go to church together. I would love it. But that is imposible now. But I hope the time will not be long distant when Peace will once more shine over this great Republic the home of the Brave and the Land of the free. But Sarah we have to contend against a Powerful foe. Dear Sarah ain't is curious that the Presidents Proclimation[2] comes into effect on my Birthday. It would be curious if Peace should be Proclamed on that day the 1st of January. But I hope it will be before. God grant it there has been enough lives sacrifised in this unholy war. Now I should think if the head men would see the suffering it [has] caused they would close it at once. But I hope for my self if it is ever settled it will be done satisfactory to Both Parties. If it aint let it go on till ether one side or the other is Anihilated. It is very strong talk but it must be so. But things sometime look dark. But the darkest Hour is just befor day. We are on the Right and god will Help us and favor our arms. We have about two or three Hundred wounded Rebels around [within] a stone throw of our camp. I go down and see them every day. There is one or two die every day. It is an awful sight. They are a dirty lousey set half clothed and raget at that. Dear Sarah I must now close for I must clean my gun and keep in good fighting trim so I can Pop a Rebel every time. So good By. God Bless you Both is my Prayer and Keep you from all harm.

I remain Your loveing Husband
John H Pardington
Co. B 24 Michigan Infantry
1st Army Corps
Gen Gibbons Brigade Washington D.C.

1. Probably John Clee, aged thirty-five, from Trenton. The proprietor of Clee General Store.

2. The Emancipation Proclamation, which came into effect on John's twenty-fourth birthday, January 1, 1863.

Wednesday Oct 23/62
Camp Pennyman
Near Bakerville M.D.

My Dear Wife

I have just received your kind and affec letter which I am sure I received with heartfelt gratitude. Well Sarah we have moved again and we have not been here only 3 days when last night about 12 oclock news came to have 3 days raitions to be cooked right off and you never say [saw] so much cooking in your life. Before the whole division numbering about 20 thousand men it was a splendid sight to see so many fires at once. I was on guard that night. We just dump right on the ground the sky over us the sod Beneath. Dear Sarah we expect to start by 12 oclock. Our next stopping plase within the face of the enemy we will have to wade across the Potomic up to our midle in water. Won't that be pleasent for fall weather I think so. But we will have to grin and Bare it. So I think that before this letter reaches you we will have changed shots with the Rebels. It might as well come first as last. Dear Wife you said I suppose I like to hear about you and the baby best. Dear Wife that is the only news I like to hear about. I could sit all day and hear from you Both and not tire me. So dear do not be afraid to tell me all about you and the dear little Creature Maria. God Bless her, and you too Dear Sarah. I have answered your two letters you spoke about. I suppose you have received them By this time now. Sarah don't be afraid to write But if you don't get a letter soon enough just sit down and write. Never mind for answers because I will answer them in good time for you know dear we are quite aways off now and still getting further all the time and I hope the Union army will winter in Richmond. Now is the time or never but it will cost an awful sight of blood before we do it. I don't want to winter anywhere But there for if we do go into winter quarters and let them get a fresh hold why it is gone up. That what I think and a good many more and I bleive it to. The troops are eager to go forward and why not Push them. Constrentate [concentrate] the whole army and sweep all before it and if it come to that drive the whole Rebel hoarde from the face of the Southern soil, so it will save the union. That my motto and all others that is true to the cause. Dear Sarah I hope this letter will find Jo better and up again. Give my love to Both of them and family and all the rest around there. I think it is curious that Maryann or Ed do not write to me. They have got more time than I have. I will answer it though if they will wright. Tell me in your next letter if luke Covill[1] has Paid you or not. If he has not do not dun him no more. But I will write him a note which I think will make him Pay for I think he has acted a mean Peice of Business after letting him come in when he though[t] best. But never mind dun him no more. Only send me word if he Pays or not. Dear Sarah we have not received any Pay yet nor don't expect to yet awhile. But mind and get your orders for the Boy[s] that live in detroit and Wyandotte their wifes [got] theres. For just as soon as we get our Pay I shall send the drafts which I subscribed for in detroit. Dear Sarah the 18 New York Reigment is here. But Elias is not joined his reigment yet. He is at Alexandria on Parole. He is not exchanged yet. Elias and Hank are well and the rest of the trenton boys. I was much obliged to you for that Peice [of] Poetry you sent me. I think it was very nice for Hattie. I received a letter from Willie and Mr Clee the same time I received yours. Me and Brother Bill write regular to one another so I think Maryann might as well write. I sent Jo a letter. I suppose he as got it by this time. Remember me to father and send mother note to her for Bill told me she was there and she sent me a kiss. So good By. Kiss Maria for me. How I would like to see her. Sarah you said true about no one wife feels nor no one knows what a Husband feel till they try it. I could not describe my feelings in ink. So Good By god Bless and Protect you Both is the Prayer from Your Loving Husband

John H. Pardington
Co. B 24 Mich Infantry
1st Army Corps
Gen. Gibbons Brigade
Washington D.C.

Now dear Write soon
and often

A Kiss

1. Probably Lucius D. Coville, a miller from Washtenaw County, Michigan.

Oct 25/62
Camp Penymen
Near Bakerville M.D.

My dearest Wife
I have just received your kind and affec letter dated Oct. 17th and glad was I to hear from you for I had the ague yesterday and was pretty sick.

But to day I feel Better only my head Pains me very bad. I think if I only had you to nurse me and bathe my head I think I should be all right in a little while. I have quite a fever on me now. But I hope when I write again I shall be over it. To morrow is my [illegible] day. If I don't have it to morrow I think I shall be over it. But Dear Wife this is a bad plase to be sick for we are moving now every week. Sometimes we do not stay only a day in a plase. I received a letter from you the other day and sent the answer right off. Dear Wife I think Mary must have felt quite ashamed when her Husband found her at a dance. I do not know how I should feel But I hope I never have the oppertunity to feel so. But from you aching so I have no fears dear, How did she know but What When she was enjoying herself on the floar to the sound of the fiddle he might have been Laying on the Battle feild wounded or dying. Shame on a Woman with no more feeling than that. She do not deserve the sacred name of Wife. I thank God that I have such a Wife as I have got. God Bless her. Sarah I Prayed for you and Baby last night till my eyes were wet with tiers and I felt much relieved. Thank thank God. How is little Maria? How I would like to see her the dear little Creature. Don't get jeligous Sarah for I love you Both. I told you in my last letter that we were going off across the Potomic at twelve oclock. But the Order seems were not right. But we expect to go every moment dear to meet the Rebels for I hear the Army is not going into winter quarters. I hope not But let us settle it up at once. For it is time it was done. For if they don't Whip them this winter we never will. Tell Mr McIlheny Jim[1] is well and sleeps and Bunks with me and we are going to stick together. He is in good health tell them. Dear Sarah you must not expect no more from me this time for there is letters you will receive before you get this that I wrote nearly all the news in up till now. Tell me if Jo got his letter. If he did tell him to answer it and I will write Back. Give my love to all at home. Kiss little Maria for me and except one loving kiss from your affec Husband

John H. Pardington
Co. B 24 Mich Infantry
1st Army Corps
Gen Gibbons Brigade
Washington D.C.

Write soon Hank send his
Best Respects to all and
Jim McIlheny

1. James McIlhiny, a "Trenton Boy" in Company B and John's best friend. He was the son of Alexander McIlhiny, a bookkeeper from Trenton, Michigan.

dear Sarah

Near Harper's ferry M.D.
Oct 29/62

My dear Wife

haveing a few spare moments to write you a few lines I thought I would do it. But Sarah you must not expect much this time for we have moved again. No troops ever differed more than we did on our last March here. We were ordered Last Sunday affternoon to Pack up and be off in three minutes notice. It [was] raining hard all the time. We started at three oclock in the afternoon and marched through mud and Rain till half Past eight at night. Dark as Pitch we halted in a feild and had to stand up all night in the rain and cold nothing But a Blanket around us. What do you think of that dear Sarah. We marched 26 miles. We are now waiting our turn to cross the Bridge of the Potomic. The whole army is moving. There will be heavy work in a few day. There must be a Big Battle here in a few days. God help the Union arms for we must conquer or die. I had a letter from Elias yesterday he is at Alexandria and well. I answered it right off. Dear Sarah this all I can write now. This aint no answers to any of your letters or I would wrote it longer. But you must excuse any more this time. So Good By God Bless you Both is the Prayer of your loveing Husband

J. H. Pardington
Co. B 24 Mich Infantry
1st Army Corps Gibbon Brigade
Washington D.C.

Send my love to all. I am looking for a letter from you every day. Kiss little Maria for me. God Bless and take one for yourself

Jack

I gues we will be off to morrow for Dixie.
Two month to day since I last saw you.
It is impossible to get my likeness taken now.

Camp Near Lovetsville
Virginia
Oct 31/62
once more in dixie

My dear Wife

haveing a few spare moments to write you a few lines I thought I would improve the oppertunity. For you Dear Sarah I delight in writing to you. But Sarah I have not recived any letters from you since I wrote to you to direct my letter to

J. H. Pardington
Co. B 24 Mich Infantry
Gen Gibbons Brigade
Washington D.C.

But dear Wife I expect them every day and am anxioux looking out for them I tell you. Now dear Sarah we have moved again and am now again in the Sacred Soil of Virginia. We are marching now to meet the enemys if they will only stop till we [catch] up with them. If they do there will be Hot work here in a few days Probily before this letter reaches you if so god favors our arms. We only stop long enough on our marches to rest the men and cook something to eat. It is splendid weather down here now as warm and as nice as our June Weather in Michigan. God grant that it may stay so on account of our army for that is what we need now for success to our arms and the glorious Stars and Stripes. For they must wave over our enimeys in success before another month Passes over. When you write tell me who is drafted. I hope they wont draft Jo for the sake of his family. How are they all. Kiss them all for me will you Sarah. Thank god I am enjoying the best of health and Spirits. Blessed be his name for his goodness toward me How is little Maria? Oh how I would like to see her the little dear. Kiss her sweet lips for me and envoke my blessing on her head. How is Mother since her visit to William? Kiss her for me and tell [her] I am well and hearty and in the best of Spirits only a little homesick once in a while. But Sarah a Husband that as [has] a Wife and child to home cant help [it] and he would be only a Brute if he had not them. I know I have them. Well dear Sarah we have a large foarce down here and I dont see what is going to hinder us from getting into Richmond this fall for I hear we are not going into Winter quarters and I hope not. Every mils now we march Brings us nearer the enemys forces. Last night or yesterdy afternoon we crossed the Potomic at Berlin six miles below Harpersferry. It was a grand sight to see us crossing the Pontoon Bridge made of Boats with Plank laid on them. The Rebels Burnt the main Bridge at the surrender of Harper. Dear Wife give my love to your Father and family. Tell him I will write to him when I get time. Sarah I must quit for we are ordered to march again.

8 oclock at night

well Sarah here we are again Halted for the night further into dixie and nearer the enimey. We may not stop till morning but I rather think we will but I think I can finnsh this before the Bugle sounds fall in. It nothing but fall in and March again all the time and it will be now till we meet the Rebels. I suppose it is cold and nasty down there now while here it is Pleasent and nice. It is a spelendid evening here. The moon shines Bright and fair and it is so warm you could sleep out with out anything But a Blanket. We are camped to night right in a Big Orchard But there is nary apple on though so we will have to look at the trees and wish. It looks nice here tonight to see so many camp fires around. If you see Mr McIlhenny tell him Jim is well and in the best of health and we both stick together like Brothers and we mean to as long as we live and if either of us get wounded we will then try to take care of one another. But I hope thank [God] that will not be the case. But the fortunes of war are singular. But he has Spared us Both so far and we thank him. Sarah I must soon cry quits for we do not know what time the bugle may sound and then wont have time to send it. So now dear Wife I must wish you a sweet good night and send you a kiss for you and the little angle Maria. God Bless her and you. Oh how I would like to see you Both and imprint one sweet kiss on your lips. But God grant that I may before long But it cant be till this unholy war is ended. So now dear I must say again good night. But I hate to for I would like and sit and write all night. But that is imposible for we need sleep and rest for we have to carry between forty and fifty pounds on our Back. I tell you Sarah I never new what hardships was before But I tell you I know now to my heart content. Give my love to all and except the same from loveing Husband

John H Pardington
Co. B 24 Michigan Infantry
1st Army Corps
Gen Gibbens Brigade
Washington D.C.

P.S. Write soon and tell me all the news. We now carry sixty rounds of cateridge apeice. But we call them Union Pills so we go prepared. Sarah it is imposible for me to get my likeness taken now for we are along ways from a artist so you will have to give up expecting it. But if I should get a chance to get I will send it. We expect to be Payed in a few day. Then I will send you what I signed for on the allotment Role in a draft. So good By God Bless you all and a kiss for all. Yours True and forever

Your Jack

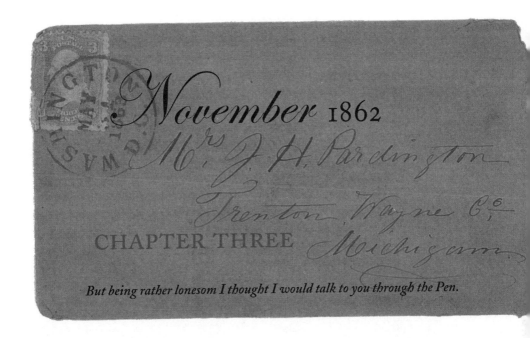

November 1862

16 J. H. Pardington

Trenton, Wayne Co.,

CHAPTER THREE

Michigan

But being rather lonesom I thought I would talk to you through the Pen.

During November, the regiment continued to march from camp to camp. When they weren't marching, they were drilling. The raw recruits were beginning to take shape. Colonel Morrow, a judge from Detroit before his enlistment and now the commander of the Twenty-fourth Regiment, had to march his troops through Warrenton, Virginia, an area known to sympathize with the Southern cause. Having been born and brought up in Warrenton, Colonel Morrow faced a special challenge.

Splendid weather greeted them. John found the countryside much to his liking; it reminded him of coon hunting at home, and he was saddened that such a lovely area should be a theater of war. Nevertheless, he, along with many others, frequently appropriated [stole!] anything they could find, such as fence rails for their campfires and food from the surrounding farms, to make their encampments more tolerable.

The overwhelming feeling among the troops was one of great anticipation that there would be fighting any day, as the Rebels were just a short distance away. In reality, their first engagement would not occur until mid-December at the great Battle of Fredericksburg. John's Company B was deployed to Potomac Creek to guard an important bridge used to transport vital supplies to the Union troops near Fredericksburg.

A major change in command occurred when President Lincoln changed the leadership of the Army of the Potomac, replacing General McClellan with General Burnside. The Iron Brigade also experienced a

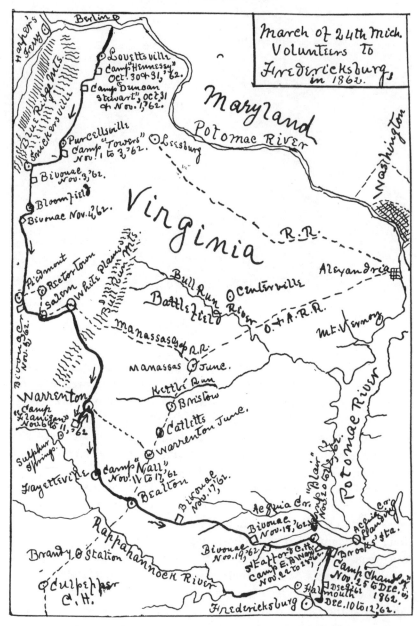

March of Twenty-fourth Michigan Volunteers to Fredericksburg in 1862.

command change; General John Gibbon, a dedicated soldier and very strict commander, stepped down in early November. Although he had his detractors, most of the men in the Brigade held him in high esteem and with affection. Colonel Morrow of the Twenty-fourth Michigan temporarily replaced him.

Optimistically, John continued to believe that the rebellion would be stamped out and that he would be home by spring.

Nov 1 1862
On Pickett
1/2 Past eleven Oclock Saturday Night
Vergenia

Dearest Wife

I received your kind and welcome letter and glad I was to read it and to hear from loved ones at home. Dear Sarah this is rather a Curious Place to write a letter But Better than none. I received your letter this morning just before we marched. I just got through reading it when we were ordered to fall in. We marched till three Oclock in the afternoon when we halted and our Company and Company G were ordered right on Picket. So you see we are not far from the Rebels. Dear Sarah it puts me in mind of coon Hunting But we are looking out for Rather Bigger game though I should like to have some of the Boys here with me that used to go a coon Hunting with me. But I tell you we have got to keep our eyes skined and not be caught a napping. This is our first trial on Picket for the 24th Mich and it is something new for us. Jim McIlheny is sleeping a little ways from me. Some sleep while some keep watch and then turn around and the other ones sleep. It is Pleasent and warm here to night and the moon shine Bright and it is Pleasent. Midnight now and all is well. We caught one or two suspicious looking fellows on our lines to night. I had to take one about a mile up to the General headquarters But he Proved all right and so we let him go. We have to be carefull and let no one in or out. If they dont Halt shoot them down. That the ways.

7 oclock Sunday Morning

Well Sarah we have Passed the night all right and here we are just got through Drinking our coffee and eating our Pork and hard Biscuts. I am well and in good spirit Thank God. We expect to march to day. We are not more than 3 or 4 miles from the enimys so I think the next Plase we fetch up will be in front of them. It is a splendid morning here so warm and Pleasent. It seems here now to look at nature that there was now war. But then come to look at our foarces and our Brass war dogs it wears then a different aspect. There was a heavy Skirmish on our Left Yesterday afternoon. The fireing was very heavy. It was about 5 miles from us. We Rekon it was at a Plase called union. A small village. It is quite a Pleasent county around here. Now dear Wife I have not much more to write at Present because we do not know what minute we may be called to fall in and be off. Dear Sarah when ever I can get time I will write a note to Covile for I think he as acted mean toward you after letting him come in when he wanted to. But that is all the thanks you get. Now Sarah write and tell me all the news you can and who is drafted or if they have commencd to draft yet. Give my love to all at home. Kiss them all for me. I wish I was down there to go to church with you and baby to day But that is imposible. So good By. God Bless you and Baby is my Prayer from Your affec Husband

J. H. Pardington

A Kiss

Co. B 24 Mich Infantry
1st Army Corp Gibbon Brigade
Washington D.C.

In Haste

Near Warrenton Virgenia
Nov 8/62

This in Haste. I write a few lines Hoping it will find you and Baby enjoying good health with [which] thank God I am enjoying myself. Dear Wife you must not expect only a few lines from me now for we are marching all the time. We arrived here the other night at twelve oclock at night. The Rebels left a few hours before us so you must know we are close on to them. There is heavy fireing ahead of us now. We expect to march every minute. We expect to be in a fight every day and every Hour. Give my love to all. We have been marching for the last week and I tell you we felt Pretty tired when we arrived here. To morrow is Sunday. I should be surprised if we had a fight to morrow it being sunday. We dont get letters so regular and often as we used to But I will write as often as I can and you the same. We had quite a snow storm here yesterday. It lasted all day and there is snow on the ground now. If you see Mr

Mclheny tell him Jim is well. So good By God Bless you is my Prayer from your Loveing Husband

J. H. Pardington
Warrenton Vergenia
Sunday Nov 10/62

My dear Wife

I have just received your Kind and Welcome letter with Baby hand in it. I am much Obligrd [obliged] to you for What you sent me. For to tell you the truth dear Sarah I needed it for we have not received any Pay yet and I do not know When we will. And Sarah you are quite right in what you said about sending one at a time. No indeed I will not call you stingy for you were never that Dear Sarah. I wrote you a short letter yesterday in lead pencil. Only a few lines and sent it off. It was no answer to any of your letters But I thought we were going off and I thought I would have no other chance for a while for when we get started there is no Knowing when we will stop. But we have not moved yet on acount of our supply train not arrivng. But it it arrived this afternoon so there is no telling what minute we may move. Dear Sarah you said about sleeping on a feather bed. To tell the truth I do not know how it would feel for I have slept in my cloths ever since I left and that night I slept with you at Williams. I could not tell how it would feel to undress go to Bed. If I ever get home God Willing I suppose I shall have to sleep outside on the ground for the first two or three nights for I do not think I could sleep in a Bed again. Give my love to all of Jos folk. Tell him I shall expect that letter from him before long. Dear Sarah you say about this war being endid. God only know when it will end. But I do not think it will be ended at the Point of Bayonette. It seems strange don't it but that is my oppinion and a good many others. I tell you Sarah they have a big foarce for they press every thing into their Ranks that can carry a gun. Every where we have Passed in vergenia you cant see a young man and hardly a old one. Nothing but niggers takeing care of there farms while they are fighting in the Ranks. I tell you Sarah they will have to draft and get such a foarce that will sweep all before it. Asking to getting into Richmond this fall I do not think any of us will see it with out we are taken Prisenors and that I dont want to be If I never see it. I had a nother letter from Elias the other day from alexandria. He is well and told me when I wrote home to send his love to all there. You said Perfectly Right about going to live at mothers this winter. I do not think it will be hardly safe for it will be very cold for you and the baby. Give my love to mother and father. I tell you Sarah I have done some hard marching this last week.

Me and Jim Mack gave out about eleven oclock at night and let the Reijment go ahead. It was about one oclock when we caught up with them. They had camped for the rest of the night. Me and Jim Passed through Warrenton all alone.[1] It['s] a regular secesh hole so we kept our eyes skined for Breakers ahead.[2] Tell Mr Mclheny that he [his son, Jim] is well and going to write him a letter directly I get through with the Pen. Now dear Sarah I have no more to write at Present. I am well and am enjoying the Best of health. Thank God he has spared me and Blessed me with health and life so far. Give my love to all and kiss Baby for me and except one from your loveing Husband, J. H. Pardington. Direct your letters as before just the same.

I send you too kisses in return for what you sent me. Good night for it is most bed time. Jim McIlheny received a letter from his mother the same time as I did this. Tell them so when Jo sees this he is going to answer it to night

Jack

1. An area populated by Southern sympathizers.
2. "Breakers" refers to guerrilla fighters.

Head Quarters 24 Mich Infantry
Near Fayettvills Virgenia
Nov 12/62

Dear Wife

Haveing a few spare moments to spare I thought I would write you a few lines wich I hope will find you Both enjoying good health wich thank God I am enjoying my self. We are still marching or Halting now all the time. We have very fine weather now since the snow storm But it is rather cloudy here to day. I should not be surprised if it would rain here before night. Dear Sarah this is no answer to any of your letters But Being Rather lonesom I thought I would talk to you through the Pen which is the only way we can communicate to one another which we ought to be thankfull we can do so. Dont you think so. Dear Sarah the only thing that Bothers me now is a stone Bruise I have got on my foot wich troubles me on a march. But the doctor gave me a Pass wich will enable me to fall out if nessary. But I have kept up so far with success. But it Pains me a good Deal on rough Roads where there is stones. Vergenia is a very deserted [state]. The part were we have Passed through. I have seen no state I like so well as I do Michigan. *Perticular around home* were loved ones are. Dear Sarah how is the little Baby Maria. How I would like to see her. She must have grown quite a large child. What is the color of [her] eyes are the[y] black. How is mother and all the folk around there. Are they well. Dear Sarah How I would like to be with you now. But I cant. So I shall have to be contented with writing to one another. Dear Sarah I have not much news to write to you for I wrote you a letter the other day and told you all the news I Knew. We are still marching on the enemys. I suppose we will soon have a Battle here which will be a most terrific one. Some think we will not have one till we get to Richmond. But I think we will have one before we get there or else I am deceived. Gen. McClellan Reviewed his troops for the last time on Monday. I suppose you will have heard of the change before you receive this. Burnsides[1] now command[s] the Army of the Patomic. Some of the old soldiers don't like it very well But we will see what Burnsides will do now. Dear Sarah I wish you would send me a newspaper containing the Account of the Returns of the Election. I would like to see it. You can get one off Willie. He will give you one. Well dear I must say good By. God Bless you Both is the Prayer of your affec and loveing Husband

J. H. Pardington
(Direct as before)

Give my love to all Jo folks and to Mother and Father
Good By

1. Major General Ambrose E. Burnside.

camp near fayettville
Head Quarters 24 Mich. Infantry
Vergenia
Nov 13/62

Dearest Wife

I have just received your affec Letter dated Nov 2 and glad I was to hear from you And Baby. I was Pained to hear about your throat being So soar. Dear Sarah do mind and take care of your self for my sake Dear. I think it was Honerable of Mr Smith in seeing of that affair. For I had forgotting all about it. It is as you say some would have Put in there pocket. When you see him thank him for me and give him my Best Respects. Dear Sarah I am enjoying good health. Thank god. Why Sarah I can almost eat a hores Hind Leg. I never get satisfied somehow or other. I want to eat all the time. Rather Pay the Butcher than the doctor dont you say so. Well you may say dear Sarah. We will know how to appreciate each other company if God Willing we should meet again. For this separation do try us. It does me and I know it do you dear for you are almost constantly in my mind and dear Sarah I Pray for you and Baby every night that God may Bless and Protect you Both and give you health and strength. Dear Sarah Pray O that I may find you a christain woman if [God] Permits me to return to you. For Sarah I love you with all my heart. But Sarah we ought not to forget our Maker who gives us health and strength dear. Sarah I do not know when this war will end. God only know but we expect a Bloody time here before many days. For we advanceing all the [time] now only when we Halt for rest. Tell Mr McIlhiny if you see him that [h]is son is well and in good health. Give my best respect to them when you see them. Dear Sarah this is splendid weather down here now just like our Michigan June weather. Why to day I was around with only one shirt on and sweating at that. It is after eight at night now and it is Pleasent night so warm and nice. Well we might call it the sunny south. It seems to bad that such a splendid country should be made the thearte of war. We burn all the rails we come accross when we camp. It would make you laugh to see us when we camp for the night to see thousands of Blue coat Soldiers runing to see who will get the most rails and I tell you the Wayne County Tigers arnt behind either. They dont beat the 24th much now I tell you. You can hardly see a rail when we leave a camp ground. I dont think Jo would like to have us camp on his farm for he would not have a fence left in the morning. That is if he was secesh. Nor straw nor Hay and he would do well if he had his house left. We make things suffer I tell you. Dear Sarah now mind and take care of your health. Ask God to give you health for it would make me feel very bad to have you sick and me so far away from you. Now dear Sarah I must say good By for there is 3 or 4 letters ahead of this for I sent them within ten days from this date. Give my love to all and may God in heaven Bless you is the Prayer of your affec Husband

John. H. Pardington

Direct your letters the same

Near fayettvile Virgenia
Sunday at noon Nov 16/62

My dearest Wife (Your letter was dated Nov 5)

I have just received you[r] True and Welcome letter. O how eager I tore open the Preacious missive which contains lines from my darling Wife and news from my sweet baby. Dear Sarah I am well and in good health. Thank God for his tender mercies toward me for I think Sarah he has been most gracious toward me since I left there. I have not been well sometimes But I think I have my health good considering the hardship we have to endure. I am sorry for Kate. I believe that Charley wants to get rid of her and have sent her home to father. I tell you dear Sarah let him come out here and miss the Presence of a loveing Wife as I do. I think he would be ashamed of himself. Oh Sarah it is true as you say in one of your letters this do try us. Dear Sarah about this war. I think as a good many more we will be home by spring. I hope to God we will for there [h]as been a nough Blood spilt [in this] unholy Rebelion. There has been no heavy fighting here yet but heavy skirmihing though about every day. The enemy are in strong foarce in our front under Jackson. We cant tell what the result will be but the army is advancing all the time. Tell Willie when you see him I had a letter Wrote to him. I had it in my Pocket. We were ordered to march it raining all the time and it got spoild in my Pocket and I had to throw it away. Tell him I will write him another in good time. Tell him I have not got that shot gun yet. Dear Sarah the Trenton Boys are all well and in good health. It was quite cold here last night. But it is Pleasent here to day. They had quite a heavy Skirmish in our front yesterday. We could hear the shells Burst quite Plain after the Report of the gun. I tell you [it] took us quite by surprise when we heard that Gen McClellan was taken away from us. But probily it is all for the Best. Burnsides is a goo[d] head man and I guess he will show the Rebels that he will do something this fall that will open their eyes. I hope so. The troops are all eager for it. Dear Sarah you must not expect a long letter from me this time for I have wrote four this week. I suppose you take care of all my letters. But I cant do that with yours for I read them over and over again and then I have to Burn them. For it would not do to carry them in case of being taken Prisoner. Give my Best Respect to all Jo folks. Sarah if you can I want you to keep Jo payed up all the time when it is due and it will then keep thing straigh[t] for Jo has been Kind to us since we have been married and if ever I can repay that Kindness I will. Give my love to mother and Kiss her good for me and all the Rest. I got a letter from Bill and Dan at Mr Parks at the same time I got yours. Dear Sarah I am very sorry for your teeth for I know what you suffered before Dear Sarah and I can now feel for you. But I hope the[y] will be better. I must now say good By. Give the Baby a kiss for me and except the same from your True and affec Husband

J. H. Pardington

May God in Heaven Bless you Both is the Prayer of your devoted

John
Write soon

dear Sarah

Dear Wife

I have just received your kind and affec letter dated Nov. 11 which brings our little darling five months old. How I would like to see her. But never mind God Willing I shall [see] her again. Dear Sarah I would like for you to write the date of my letter on yours every time you write an answer to mine for your letters are so long a coming that I dont think you get all my letters. What is the reason I got a letter from George my Brother and here it is 16 days your comeing to me. They cannot send the letters from the Post office for your letters date and theirs on the envelope dont agree together. I wish you [would] speak to them about it and tell them to send them as quick they can go out. For if I dont get a letter once a week from you I begin to feel uneasy about you. Dear Sarah last Tuesday made quite a change in our Reigment. We are detailed now to gaurd the Railroad which runs from Fredericksburg to Aquia Creek. Our Company are within 6 or 7 miles of Fredericksburg gaurding a Bridge. The bridge was burnt down and they are now building it and will have it finished to morrow. We may have to stay here all the winter and we may not stay a week but I think we will stay. It is a good job for we dont have to march any. Our Reigment extends 7 miles. There tow [two] important Bridges to gaurd. For when the army moves again no doubt the Rebels will try and destrow [destroy] the Bridges. So you see Company B [h]as got the Post of Honer. So much for us. Now Sarah you said you were going to detroit. Now get the Babys likeness taken good for I would like to have it and your too. For O Dear I do want to see you so bad. Sometimes I get so lonsome. But I will drive it away again Kiss your picture and Babys and then feel all right. But then it wont Kiss me Back again. So it is not like you for you will kiss me when I kiss you. But never mind dear. Let us Put our trust in God and all will be well. Dear Sarah I Pray for you often. Yes every night. Do you for me. I know you do dear and my wish is Dear Sarah and my Prayer that when I return it will be to find you a Christian woman and a praying one. For if I do return to you again my vow is to let Whiskey Profane Swearing and the like forever Behind for dear Sarah I have quit them all *now*. Sarah no one hears me now uter an oath and I dont think they will. For with God help I will succeed. Pray for me dear Sarah that I may. Sarah I have learnt a lesson since I left you. My concience [h]as smote me more than once for my Past life and I am Bound to reform. Dear Sarah I have my health first rate. I was never was Better in health and Spirits. Sarah I want you to send me a Pair of gloves Buckskin. We have not received any Pay and it make it very unpleasent for us for I tell you we get short sometimes and dont get enough to eat. But about the gloves. Young Hollstead[1] had a Pair sent to him to day from trenton. You find out by Mary Hollstead and send them the same way. And tobaco is awful scarce. We do not no what to do with our selves for the want of it. I tell you a few Plugs would be quite acceptible. I tell you Enclosed I send you some cotton in it native state. I could not send it stem an all. The Husk on it is good deal like a shuck on a Hickory nut in the fall when it Burst and the nut ready to fall out. We picked this on one of our last marches on a Plantation. This is the Pure state it grows in. Now dear I must say good By. Dont forget the gloves for it is getting quite cool nights when we are on gaurd. Handling the gun gives us cold fingers But it is nice and Warm days. I must now come to a close. Give my kind [regards] to All and Except the same from Your Affec Husband

John H. Pardington

Direct your letters the same
Write soon Write soon

P.S. did you ever receive a letter from me one I wrote when I was on Pickett since we have been in Vergenia write and tell me

King Cotton

I had to Pick this to Peices in order to get it in the letter there is one or two seeds in it

Jack

1. Nathaniel A. Halstead, aged twenty, another "Trenton Boy" in Company B and formerly a farmer. He was the son of Benjamin and Aurelia Halstead.

Sat Nov 29/62
Patomic Creek Station
Near Freericksburg
Virgenia

Dear Father

I am allmost ashamed to write to you. But I know you will forgive me for I tell you we have a good deal to do. But Father I have been neglegent in not writing to you But I ask your forgiveness. Now for a little news from the Gallant 24th. Well Father we are Detailed to guard the Railroad from Aquia Creek to the Patomic Creek Station. Our Company

dear Sarah

CoB has got the Post of Honor being nearest the enemys. Our Reigment extends some seven miles so you see they streetgh[stretch] quite aways in length. Our Company as got quite an importance Plase to gaurd in the shape of a Bridge which croses the Creek here. It is about 3 or 4 Hundred feet long and about 80 feet High. It was Burnt down awhile ago. But our [forces] have rebuilt it. They finesh it the other day and the cars run now to falmouth oppisit Fredericksburg which is of great importance to us in carrying supplies to our troops in front of Fredericksburg. We will have to keep a sharp lookout for the Bridge when our army moves again for I shouldent wonder if the Rebels should make a raid on it. If they do we will meet them with our Springfeilds and Union Pills as we call our Bullets. Well Father it is splendid weather down here now something like our june weather in Mich. Only a little cold night But splendid days. How do you like the change in Millitary affairs. I think it is all for the Best if they will only let Burnsides do What he likes. I think he would settle the Rebellion for he is a fighting man dont you think so. Father give my love to all at home. I get letters from Sarah and daughter which thank god allways Brings good news of her health. Father I must Bring this to a close in Order to send it by mail. So good By God Bless you. This from

Affec Son
J H Pardington

Write soon
    Co. B 24 Mich Infantry
    1st Army Corps
    Gibbon Brigade
    Washington D.C.

I had no stamp

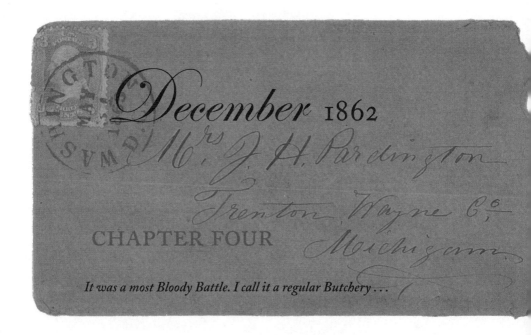

December 1862

CHAPTER FOUR

It was a most Bloody Battle. I call it a regular Butchery . . .

Problems developed in December. The weather was bitterly cold and rainy, and sickness worsened. Several members of the Regiment died because of lack of medicines and food, and after the Battle of Fredericksburg, some died of the exposure they had suffered as they lay wounded and unattended on the battlefield. One of the dead, James Nowlin, was the oldest member of the regiment; having passed himself off as forty-three at his enlistment, he was actually seventy years of age.

A dense fog covered the land on Saturday morning, December 13, hiding the deployment of the Federal divisions. When the fog lifted, they were in plain view of the Confederate troops. It was such a sight that General Lee was heard to say, "It is a good thing that war is so terrible, or we would grow overfond of it." The battle was fierce, and the men of the Twenty-fourth finally "saw the elephant" (a Civil War expression for being shot at). The weeks of drilling paid off for Colonel Morrow as he finally proved to the rest of the Iron Brigade that his men were brave and courageous fighters, not "bounty men." Major Dawes of the Sixth Wisconsin glowingly commended them: "The Twenty-fourth made a good appearance in this, their first engagement. No soldiers faced fire more bravely, and they showed themselves of a fiber worthy to be woven into the woof of the Iron Brigade."

There were no real military gains by either side in the Battle of Fredericksburg, but there were major gains for the regiment. They had

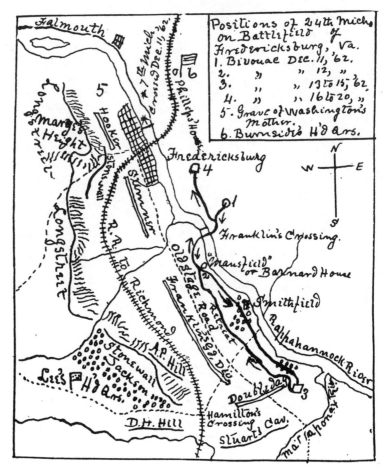

The map shows positions with the following legend:

Positions of 24th Mich. on Battlefield of Fredericksburg, Va.
1. Bivouac Dec. 11, '62.
2. " " 12, "
3. " " 13 to 15, '62.
4. " " 16 to 20, "
5. Grave of Washington's mother.
6. Burnside's Hd Qrs.

Positions of Twenty-fourth Michigan on Battlefield of Fredericksburg, Virginia.

earned the acceptance of the rest of the great Iron Brigade and were now eligible to wear with honor the famed black hats. Sadly, there were also losses. The first man was killed in action. In total, thirty-six men of the Twenty-fourth were killed or wounded, while the combined losses of the other regiments of the Iron Brigade stood at thirty-three.

John was very lucky; he had come through the battle unscathed and was enjoying good health, free of the persistent disease plaguing the troops. Before the fighting, he had asked Sarah for a much-needed pair of gloves, and he had sent her a draft for $13.50, the first pay they had received. John was "out of spirits" because they had to retreat.

Sarah's brother, Elias, joined John for a visit. It was a wonderful interlude for the young men to be together and reminisce about home. This visit buoyed John's low spirits and helped prepare him for the lonely holidays ahead. The regiment's Christmas dinner consisted of boiled rice with a little molasses on it. Supper that night was hardtack and coffee.

Although quite ill with a cold he had contracted after Christmas, John sent Sarah a special drawing commemorating their second wedding anniversary on December 29. He was lonely, sad, and full of love for her. The regiment was moving into winter quarters, and the troops were ready for a much-needed rest.

Brooks Station
Vergenia
Dec 4/62

My dear Wife

I have just received your affec letter which contained your two Precious likenesses which I tell you Sarah made me feel lonesome when I gased on your lovely face and Babys I think it is a splendid Picture of yourself. Dear you are getting *fat. Women general[ly] do when their Husband leaves them for a spell.* No insult dear. They say here that I am getting fleshy so I suppose I shall have to take that reason to myself. Well I have my health thank God first rate. So far it is getting very cold here now nights but very warm days. Your likeness lays here before me now and looks so natural. *Oh Sarah* two men belonging to our Reigment is dead. They are to be buried today. One of them is a Old man By the name of Sime Miller [Simon Miller] he lived below the Rock. I guess Joe knows him and the Other one a young man by the name of Locy [Loosee] he lives up on the State line. I wonder if he is some relation to that Locy we saw at joes. There is two more I think will not live through the day. Its awful to think that they die away from friends and home. I thank God that he has gave me such good health and spirits, *thanks Be to his name* For Oh dear Sarah God keep me from the Hospital. Well Sarah we are gaurding the railroad yet. But Col Morrow is so anxious to get in a fight that I dont think we will stay here long. But I dont think he [k]now [when] he is well off for there is some of these Col. if they could get a

dear Sarah

star on their shoulder would sacrifice half their reigment. But where duty call we must go. Ira Fletcher [h]as not been well. But he is getting Better now. I am much obliged to you for that dollar you sent me. We have not received any Pay from the government yet. When we do I will send you the drafts if we get them. If not the money. Remember to Mr Smith tell him I am much obliged to him. Dear Sarah I would like to send you my likeness But there is no Plase where we can have it taken. But the first chance I can get it I will send it for I know you would like it. I have got whiskers all over my face now. But I guess you would know me dont you. How do you like the Presidents Message. I think it is all sound. I wrote your Father a letter the other day. I was almost ashamed to write not haveing wrote before But I asked his forgiveness. Sarah when you see my father tell him I think it is hard in him not answering my letter. Give my love to mother and kiss her for me. Kiss the little darling Maria for me. God Bless her. Sarah I must bring this to close. Excuse this short letter for I will write a longer one the next time God Willing. Good By God Bless and Protect you Both is the Prayer of your affec Husband and Father

John H Pardington

A kiss
Direct the same as before Write soon Write soon

God Bless you.
John

Excuse this writing for my Pen was Bad

early Tuesday morning
Brooks Station Va
head quarters 24th Mich Infantry
Dec 9/62

My dear Wife

I have just received your kind and affec letter and was very glad to hear from you and Baby. I was very sory to hear that the scarlet fever was around there again. I heard it before I got your letter that Gibbe was taken down sick with it at joes. Sarah be careful for my sake. Tell Jo that I was much obliged to him for his letter and I will answer it as soon as I can. We are under marching Orders to be ready at a moments notice and I will do well if I have time to write this before we fall in. We were gaurding the railroad But our Col is so ambitious that nothing must do but to be in a fight. There will be something done in a day or two now. Dear Sarah I feel very Proud about my Baby being Praised so. But By its picture I see it is some Baby after all. George told me in his letter that he heard it was the Best of the Pile. O how I do want to see it and Perticular you dear. We have had quite Bad luck in our Reigment lately. We have Buried seven. I should say six. There is one to be buried today.[1] Poor fellows so far away from home and friends. But it is Poor Plase here for a man when he is sick. Dear Sarah I have been very well so far only I dont feel very well sometimes but on the whole I have had my health very good. Thank God. Now Sarah Please send me a sheet of paper and a envelope when you write for I do not know what I should have done in answering this letter if you had not sent me this sheet. How I should like to be there on the 29th day of December.[2] You know that day dont you Dear. It is very cold here now. About as cold as I have seen it [in] Michigan. So dont forget to send me the gloves for I need them the worst way. We have not received any Pay yet. Give my best respects to all at home. I have not much news to write for nothing have transpired new since i wrote you the last letter But I hope the next letter. Give my love to mother when you see her. I wrote Maryann a letter the Other day. I hope she will answer it. I wrote one in order to see if she would write one for I think Ed has acted mean in not writing to me. I think Father did not do write [right] in not answering that letter I wrote him. Tell him I think it hard of him. Ira Fletcher is better than he was. All that troble me is a Pain in my side and Back. I guess the Reason lying so much on the ground. Even in this cold weather we do not have even straw to lay on. Nothing But the ground and a thin tent over us that you can see through. It seems a wonder to me that there aint more die than what there is. It is a sad sight to go to a Soldier funeral. I could not help but shed a tear in Witness of the departed one. God give the Widow strengh to Bear her Misfortune when the sad tiding reach her. Well Sarah I shall be glad when this war is over, for we have to undergo a good many Hardships. Dear Sarah now do write often and long for you do not know how a letter from you cheers me in my lonsome hours. Dear Sarah I must now bring my letter to a close with kind love to all. Kiss the Baby for me and one for your self and Believe me to be your Ever True and Faithful Husband

J. H. Pardington

Direct your letter the same

Write soon, Write soon

My Prayer is May God Bless you Both and Keep you from all decease [disease] and sickness. Sarah there is quite a change in me since I left you which I thank God for it.

Pray for me dear. Good By from your
John

Enclose is a draft—$13.50 God Bless You

dear Sarah

North side Rappahnack
Dec 16
Near FrederickBurgh

Dear Wife

Before you receive this you will know no doubt of the great Battle[1] and Retreat of our foarces and Sarah it is a defeat. Thank God I have come out safe though our foarces suffered teberall and lucky enough for us that we left as we did for had we staid there another day they would completly destroyed our army. For we had no chance with them no how. So we had to skedadle but retreat was the last thing in my mind. We retreated in the night. We were on the left of our grand army. Our reigment kept the advance all the time. Our Reigment suffered some from shell and canster and grape. We lost about 19 or 20 killed and wounded. There was three men struck down along side of me. But the 24th has got its name up I tell you. The way it stood under such a terrible fire of shoot and shell. Now dear Sarah you must not expect a long letter this time. This is only to let you know that I am safe. Thank God in him I Put my trust. We do not know what will be the result of this defeat. But know army in the world could drive them from their stronghold. Dear Good By God Bless you is the Prayer of your affec Husband

J. H. Pardington

P.S. Sarah I sent you a draft about a week ago. Have you received it. Write and tell me. You will have to sign your name on the Back of it when you want to get it cashed. Sarah I am out of spirits. Retreat was the last thing we thought off. I dont care how quick they compromise this thing. Our loss reported at 20,000 Killed and Wounded. Write soon. Kiss the Baby for me. Give my love to all

Your for ever
John

Direct as before

We are drawn up in line of Battle this side of the river. I think we are covering the retreat.

Good By

I have just received a letter from you dated Dec 6. I was very Pleased with it was the best letter I have received from you. But I cant answer it yet. I will before long God willing.

Your
Jack

1. The Battle of Fredericksburg.

Headquarters
Camp Near Fredericksburg
24 M.I.
Dec 21/62 Va

Dear Wife

Yesterday I received your [letter] dated Dec 11 and Happy I was to hear from you and daughter. God Bless you Both. I am enjoying firstrate health thank God at Present. I suppose you have heard of the Battle we were engaged in which I came out all right. I had two very narrow excapes But thank God he protected me so far. It was a most Bloody Battle. I call it a regular Butchery to take men there w[h]ere they could not get no chance with them. It is a wonder they did not cut our army all to Peaces. If we had staid there another day they would have done it and no mistake. But we retreated in the night and well we did. I do not know what will be done next. God only knows. But I wish we were into quarters for this laying on the ground so cold as it is now wont Pay much longer for we will be all down sick for it is awful cold here now. I received those gloves the same time I got your letter and a letter from your Father and I tell you they come handy. Send you a Kiss for them And will give you one when I get home. I saw Elias yesterday and had a long talk with him. He looks firstrate and healthy. He wanted one of your Pictures But I told him I could not Part with them on any account. I would not for the world. He told me to give his love to all at home. He thinks he ought to be quite Proud to be uncle to such a Baby. *I think so to.* Now Sarah dear you must Keep Christmas and New Years for me and Perticular the *29 of December.* God Bless the day I ever gave my hand and heart to you daer. We lost very heavy in this last fight. The Papers say 13000 But I think 15000. A Battle feild is an awful sight. I never want to see another but I suppose we will have to before long. No Indeed Sarah I do not laugh at you for Wanting me to Write Husband and Father. More like I ought to be shamed of my self for not doing it in respect to that dear little angel and yourself. Forgive me wont you dear. I know you will Sarah. Write and tell me if you have received that draft I sent you. They did not Pay us two months wages. If they had I would have sent you 18.00 draft. They owe us now most two months Pay near. Remember my Birthday new Years. I should like to be there but I cant. I am glad Belinda has got home for it will be more Company for you. Now tell father when you see him if he cant find a few spare moments to write to me I shall do the same. Maryann has not wrote to me yet. But thank God I have two that is most dear to me on hearth [earth] I can write to and they to me. *Sarah* Sarah I cant write no more for it so very cold here. Last night we slept in the open air only our blankets over. So you will excuse more now for my fingers ache with cold. Give my love to all and my God in heaven Bless and Keep you Both from decease [disease] and sickness is the Prayer of your affec Husband and Father

John H Pardington

Direct the same
write soon
your letters just suit me

Camp Near Fredericksburg
Dec 23/62Va

Dear Wife and Sister

It is with Pleasure we both join and Pen a few lines to you which I hope will find you and that little darling as you call her well which thank God finds me and Elias at Present. Last night Elias took you Plase along side of me in bed. I hope you will not be jealous for he makes a firstrate bedfellow. He received your letter and was Pleased to hear from you. It found him injoing good health and spirits and [he] came out all right in the late engagement. He received a letter from Father, all hands and the cook and one in Perticular which I shall not name for the Present. You will Probily hear of *her* if I return from the war. Me and Jack had a very good time together in general talking about old times and the girls in Perticular. I hope we will Both have the Pleasure of seeing home together and those we love with us. Now Sarah we have just had one of the gayest old time on record since we have met together. If we go into winter quarters close together you can set your mind we will have some fun. You must mind and eat Plenty for us Both of us on new year and christmas. Elias thinks some of going on Mary Plase when he returns safe and sound from the war. (Sarah I have had a distant entroduction to your and my new sister that will be) no doubt if he gets home safe. Elias time is not far from being ended. 4 months and a stump as I [re]call. Sarah I wish mine was as close to an end but never mind all will be well. Elias entend coming home to Michigan as soon as his time is up. Hank and Ira are well and the rest of the Michigan Boys as well as the new York Boys We will Both have to Part again this morning for our Reigment is under Marching Order to march at 1/2 Past nine. But I guess we will find one another again before long. When we get into winter quarters and get settled we are both going to send for a Box together and mind it will be a good one not to forget to Put a little Tobaco smoking and chewing. But dont send the Box till we send for it for we will write and tell you when to send it. You must now excuse any more at Present for it is time for me to Pack up and Elias Back to his camp. For he [has] several miles to go. You must now give our Kind love to all and except the same from your affec Brother Husband and Father

Father
Elias Knapp
John H Pardington

Write soon

Direct your letters as usual To Both of us. Kiss the Baby for Father and Brother.

Near Belle Plane, Va
Dec 24/62

Dear Wife

Haveing a chance to write a few lines to you for I am never tired of writing to you and sending them By James Haven[1] I thought I would emprove the oppertunity. Me and Elias wrote you one together yesterday. I hope we will be close by one another this winter for he is firstrate company. But every time I see him or talk to him it makes me feel homesick and low spirited. You can tell the reason for when ever I look at him I think of you more. Never mind dear Sarah the time may and hopes will soon arrive when I shall once more clasp and emprint a Kiss on your lips and that little darlin. God speed the day. May God of heaven Protect you Both. Dear Sarah No one knows the feeling of a Husband and Father away from home and everything looks so discouring and dark that I am almost sick and tired of it. But thank God I have my health good but I cant say about my spirits just now. But dear I shall be all right again in a day or two for I cant help it sometimes feeling so. Now dear Sarah write to me often for you can tell how I love to read these Precious lines from you. Dear Sarah one thing going off has made me a different man and I thank God for it. God willing I should return to you and Baby may the remainder of my life be spent in such a way that may be right in his sight is my Prayer. And O dear Sarah Pray for me two. I Pray for you and Baby every night as I lay down for God to keep you Both in health and spirits. Sarah I did not think a man could love a woman so as I love you today. And God Bless the day that you gave me your heart and hand. O that the time was come when I could clasp them once more to my breast but keep up spirits dear for your John sake. I have not receved any letter from you yet if you have received that draft or not. Jim McIlhenny received a letter from his father stateing that he had received his draft and we both sent them at the same time. I am anxious to hear from you about it. Tomorrow is Christmas. Our[s] will be a dull one. I wish you a merry one and a happy New Year. Well Sarah as I wrote you before we have been in battle and God Protected. But no one know the feeling of a man just before he go in. He thinks of home and loved ones for about ten minutes and then his mind is absorded in the excitement of Battle. I cant write no more. Give my love to all. May God of Heaven Bless you Both is the Prayer of your affec Husband and Father

John H. Pardington
A Kiss from John

Direct the same

1. Cpl. James Havens of Company B, and one of the "Trenton Boys."

Dec 29th 1862
Near Belle Plain
Landing
Va

Dear Wife

Last night I received your Welcome letter dated Dec 22 and very glad I was to hear from you and Baby. Your letter found me enjoying very Poor health at Present. I took with a very severe cold the day after Christmas. It has settled on me and my bones and chest. I have very uneasy nights But last night I slept some better. But I am not fit for duty yet but I hope in a few days to be around again. O Sarah the other night I thought of you when I was suffering so much Pain. If I was only I thought where you could take care of me I would soon get Better. I went to the Hospetal yesterday to get some medecine. One look was enough for me. God forbid that I should have to go there. Now dear Sarah I dont want you to Fret your self to much for I thought it my duty to tell you how I was. Jim McIlhinny waits on me and he makes a very good nurse. Sarah that letter you received of me dated Dec 9th did you not receive an allotment draft. We were Payed a little about a month and a half Pay which brought the draft to $13.50. You did not mention it in your letter. It is curious. I thought Probily you had forgot to mention it. write in your next and tell me. You never tell me how you got on with your orders. If you have received any more or not. The news you heard about CoB receiveing no injury in the last engagement was false for we had one killed and two wounded. The young fellow that was Killed was David Reed. He used to stay around where your Father lives he went to school one winter up there. He was a nice young fellow, he was only about 3 feet from me when he got struck down. I am sorrow for Old Tim Chamberlin but so much for Whiskey. Coming here has cured me. I think if I ever get home that no one will ever see me raise whiskey to my mouth only in case of necessity. Now Dear Sarah I shall not tell you of how I got the news of the scarlet fever being to Joes. Why did you not tell me. You say that I had enough to worry me But Sarah never Keep nothing from me for I always like to know the worst but I am very thankful it was no worse than it was. I received a letter from Raynor the same time I got yours and I must answer it directly I finish this. The army is doing nothing yet but we cant tell what minute we move. I hope we wont till I get Better because I do not think I could stand it to march. I am trubled with a Pain in my side considerable. This soldiering make an old man of a young one. You can feel it in your bones. When you Put on your coat a fellows arms feel stiff and sore. Sarah about sending me a box. I do not know what to say about [it]. We do not know what minute we may move and I dont want you to go to the expence of getting it up and then we not get it. But I tell you I would like one for I do not know How Butter and such things taste. How are those strawberry Preserves. Now about our Christmas dinner. We had a little Boiled Rice with a spoonful of molasses on it. That was quite a dinner was it not. That was all for supper hard Tack and coffee. You asked me if it cheers me any to get a letter from you. Dont ask me. Sarah dear if you would only see my looks when the mail came in and no letter from my two Pets at home you would think so. Now Sarah I must say good By and may heavens choiset blessing rest upon you Both is the Prayer of your affec Husband and Father

John H. Pardington

Direct your letters the same
A Kiss for Baby and you

dear Sarah

I tell you in my next letter about the Box

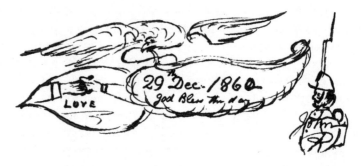

[John sketched the above picture to commemorate their wedding date, December 29, 1860]

Fryday night
Camp Near Belle Plain
10 oclock
Dec 29/63[62] Va

Dear Father[1]

I have just received your welcome letter and was glad I tell you to hear from you. Your letter found the trenton Boys all well except myself. I took a voilent cold which I am afraid has settled on my lungs. I received a Bottle of Medecine from Sarah which I hope will do me some good but I am afraid one bottle wont cure me. But I hope it will. I have not done any duty since I was first taken down. But I suppose you have heard of it before By Sarah. I hated to tell her but I thought it my duty to tell her. She must not feel alarmed about me. Col flanigan[2] arrived tonight. Elias was here today. He got a letter from you this morning. He told me there was a Pair of gloves coming for him in care of Col Flanigan which was to be left in my care. Elias will probily be over to morrow for them. If he does not I will take good care of them for him. I tell you Father it is real Pleasent to be so situated that we can visit one another. We are only six miles apart. Adue for the night for the drums has beat ta too along while ago. So good night more in the morning

Saturday A.M.

I have just got Elias gloves which I will see that he has safe. There was a whole lot of goods for the Reigment But now for me. Say Father I am going to try to get a furlough for a few weeks. That is if I do not get any better. But say nothing to Sarah about it for if I dont get it she would be dissapointed and feel Bad. So if I do get it I will kind of take her by surprise. It is Pretty hard to get one now But I will try. You was asking me to tell you about the Boys that were. [killed?] I dont know the Boys names but I know the Cap of Co K that is Cap White[3] lost his son. He was killed By a shell. Cap White has gone home. Their 2nd Leuiftenant was Killed and so the company falls in command of Leuif [Lieutenant] Wallice[4] which I believe is well. F. Forbes[5] is well as can be expect. He got struck on the shoulder By he thinks a Peice of a shattered gun. He is doing well as can be expected. Ira[6] and Henry are well and the rest of the boys. I must now say good by give my love to all and except the same from your affec son

J. H. Pardington
Co. B 24 Mich Infantry
1st Division 1st army Corp
Washington D.C.

Write soon

I feel a little better today thank God. I expect Elias here today. For my next letter I will give you an account of the Battle. John

I was took with my cold the day after Christmas. Kiss my little darling for me when you see it. Father I would like know the reason my own Father dont write to me. He has not wrote me a letter since I have been out. I think it Hard.

1. Sarah's father, Benjamin Fairchild Knapp, of Brownstown, Michigan.
2. Lt. Col. Mark Flanigan, second in command of the Twenty-fourth Michigan, and in private life a butcher from Detroit.
3. Captain William W. Wight, Commander of Company K, and in civilian life a farmer from Livonia, Michigan.
4. First Lt. Walter H. Wallace of Company K, a former student from Flatrock, Michigan.
5. Probably refers to Fernando D. Forbes, a private in Company K, and in civilian life a farmer from Brownstown, Michigan.
6. Ira Fletcher, a corporal in Company K, and in civilian life a clerk from Flatrock, Michigan.

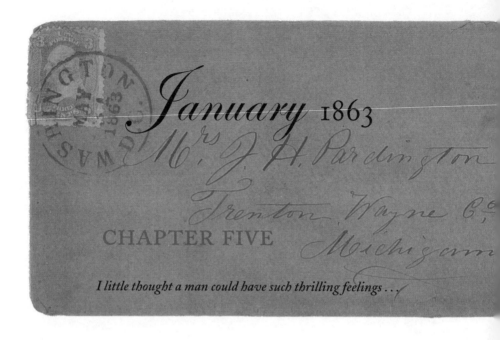

CHAPTER FIVE

January 1863

I little thought a man could have such thrilling feelings . . .

The regiment moved into winter quarters at Camp Isabella, named for Colonel Morrow's wife, at Belle Plain, Virginia. The men built log cabin–style shanties, and the Twenty-fourth, having been blessed with many farmers, taught the city dwellers how to hew logs. However, serious illness persisted, and morale was at rock bottom. On New Year's Eve, Chaplain William C. Way wrote,

> The hour and circumstances are indeed solemn. It is almost midnight and all is still save the sound of the mournful wind, whose wintry moans are a fit requiem for the dying year. In camp here, we have buried two of our men, Joseph Gohir and Marcus Wheeler of Company F. Exposure on the battlefield without blankets has multiplied our sick. We have for hospital use a loghouse and two large tents with stoves, and straw for bedding, but a lack of proper remedies and food. It is hard for a well man to live on hardtack, but too much for a sick one. It is almost impossible to get medical stores, and the lives of our men are often sacrificed for lack of them.

Major changes occurred mid-month. On January 10 and 11, Lieutenant Colonel Flanigan arrived with cartloads of mail, food, clothing, and medical supplies, and promotions for many men, including John. He was now a corporal, and his health was finally improving. He told Sarah

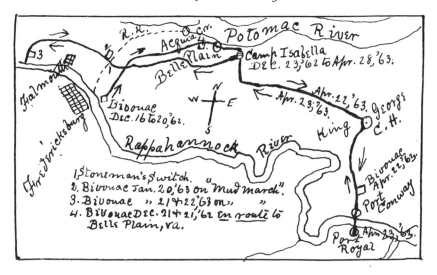

Mud March and Port Royal Expedition.

that he would like a commission but that he would have to "earn it by hard fighting."

The mail eventually brought long-overdue letters from Sarah, prompting John to reply, "Sarah I little thought a man could have such thrilling feelings for a Woman as I have for you."

Just as their circumstances were improving, General Burnside ordered the Iron Brigade to march. On January 20, they left winter quarters to once again engage the enemy and attempt to restore Burnside's reputation. The attempt failed miserably. Torrential rains turned the denuded hillsides into a sea of mud, locking mules, horses, and wagons into the mire. After spending the night in utter misery on the ground, covered only by their blankets, the men were ordered back to camp and their warm, cozy shanties. The infamous Mud March was over.

Toward the end of the month, General "Fighting Joe" Hooker replaced Burnside. Desertions were rampant: 85,123 from the Army of the Potomac had deserted by the end of January. General Hooker decided to institute a system of furloughs for the homesick men. Severe and humiliating discipline also discouraged more desertions. Some men had their heads shaved and were drummed out in front of the whole brigade.

Using some money Sarah sent him, John bought biscuits, cheese, and dried herring. His health had taken a downturn with the onset of bloody dysentery, and he badly needed something other than hardtack and pork. He encouraged her to go away with the baby for a change but to be sure his letters were saved.

The regiment would spend the next three months in its relatively comfortable winter quarters.

Friday morning Near Belle Plane
Va
Jan 2/63

Dear Wife

You must excuse much writing. I am no Better Sarah. Send me $15.00 in Haste. My lungs are very weak. But I am not in the Hospetal and I will not go If I can help it. Dont be alarmed about me. I have very bad nights. Last night was the only time I have slept a little for 5 nights and you fancy how near wore out I am I cough so much that my chest and bowels are awful sore. Elias was over to see me. He could not stay all night. He will be over again in a few days. He says he will fetch me over a Pie. My voice [h]as been good till to day and to day it is very low. Sarah this makes five letters I have wrote since the Battle. I have received no answer yet to them. I have not received only four letter from you in the month of December. What is the reason Dear Sarah. I received one from you a few days ago but that was the answer to the one before we went into Battle. I Put a draft in it which you spoke nothing about. Jim Mac father received his safe. Have you mine. Dear Sarah I will send the money Back if I dont use it. But I hope I will have to use it. Good By and may God Bless you all. Kiss little Maria for me. I cant write no more. This from your loveing

Husband and Father
J. H. Pardington

Direct the same

Write in Haste. Remember me to all.
John

I am looking anxious for a letter to night from you.

P.S. 9 oclock at night the mail has come but the long looked for letter has not come. O Dear Sarah what shall I do. Well I must lay down and try and sleep. Sarah I feel little easier to night. My cough is worse than it was through the day. Good night I hope I shall sleep good to night

Yours John
Saturday morning

I am a little Better but I had a Poor night

John

Near Belle Plane
Va
Jan 6/63

Dear Wife

I have just received your letter dated Dec 28. I was Pleased to hear from home once more. You do not know how dissapointed I have been for the last four or five mails till last night it came. But I had gave up looking for it for Sarah I have wrote 5 letters since we came of[f] the battle feild and the one I got this morning is the only answer I have got. Sarah I think you only write when you get a letter from me and then you answer it and so on. Now dear Sarah never wait for an answer but set down any time and write me a good long letter. For you dont imagen how a letter cheers me when it is from you. I dont care about a letter from any one else But you. Now Sarah I know you have got more time to write than *I have*. Now do dear let me see letters come a little oftener than what they do from you. Now Sarah dear a little news about my self. I wrote you a few days ago about how sick I had been. This morning find me a little better in spirits. My cold aint no better. I have such a bad cough I cant lay down night for hours. Cough cough all the time till one or two o clock in the morning. My cough is awful dry. I cant spit with it. My chest and Bowels get awful sore through coughing so much. Now Sarah I want you to tell me if you have received a draft of $13.50 cents from me or *not*. I sent it to you the day before going into Battle. The other boys sent theirs the same time as I did mine and they have got safe and have got answers to tell they arrived safe. I begin to feel a little anxious about it. Now do for goodness sake write and tell me you got the letter. You say it was dated dec 9th and it is curious you say nothing about the draft. If you have got it if you want to get the cash on it take it to detroit. You will have to endorse your name on the back of it because it is one of those allotment drafts no one can draw the money on them But you. If you draw it dont forget to take that certificate I gave you in detroit with you so to show them I am in the Reig and a Soldier. Now Sarah about sending your letters. Dont send another sheet of Paper inside for it costs you every time you send a letter 9 cents. You can save three. Dont send a sheet of Paper. Just send an envelope. I will find Paper so you will save a stamp on every letter. Putting so much in your letters makes them so Bulky that any body would think they were full of money. But dont forget to write a good long letter though. I think that must be some of a baby by the [way] you talk and Praise her. That is all right. Sarah how do you get along with your Orders. You never write and tell me. I do not know what is the reason But such things as that I would like to hear about very well. Sarah you say you do not feel very [well] setting up so much. Take care of yourself. I must say good by with kind love to all. Kiss baby for me and may God bless you both is the prayer of your affec Husband and Father

J. H. Pardington
Direct the same

Jan 11/62 Va
Near Belle P.

Dear Wife

I send you this note enclosed in a letter Jim McIlhenny sent to his father. We have wrote for a Box which is to be sent to Both of us. The things to be sent to Both of us in one Box. We have been chums since we have been out so whats mine is jims and what jims is mine so there is no danger of quarrel. Now Sarah dont forget to Put your share of the good things in. The reason why I send this note in jim letter is you would get it quicker than if I sent it to you By mail. We will give you a list of what we most need and what will Keep Best. I am getting Better fast. The Bottle of medicine you sent me is done me a good deal of good. I have receved no letter from you lately. I am looking anxious for one. Mr McIlheny will give you the list of what we mostly want sent. You had better go up and see them before you Prepare any thing. Sarah I want some of them Strawberies Preseves if you have any and some fine cut Tobaco. This is all I have to say Good By God Bless you all

I remain Your
affec Husband & Father
J. H. Pardington

Near Belle Plain
Jan 17/63
Va

My dear Wife

I received your Welcome and loveing letter which I received a heart overflowing with love for you and that little darling. God Bless you Both is the earnest Prayer of your affectionate Husband and Father. Sarah I wrote to you the other day how sick I was. Thank God Sarah I am better. I received that Bottle of medecene you sent me and I tell you dear it was a God send. I do not know what I should have done without it for I wont depend on these army doctars to cure me. I was greatly afraid you will be troubled about me but thank God dear Sarah I am better and to morrow I am going to try and go on drill again, for I have not been able to do any duty for 20 days. I never had such a severe cold in my life before.

Sarah do not be afraid to tell me your troubles. But God knows my heart aches and Bleeds for you when I hear it. Do they use you well to Joes. Tell *me* Sarah. Keep nothing Back as you value my happiness for I could not contain my self here if I knew you were not used well. Sarah try Mothers a spell. Tell her it is my wish and I know for her John sake she would love to have you there and another thing you could get your letters better for there is always somebody going to trenton on that road. For I tell you Sarah I would like to get them a little oftner from you for you little know my anxiety to hear about you. Sarah I little thought a man could have such thrilling feelings for a Woman as I have for you. *Sarah I love and adore you.* Sarah take care of yourself for that *little ones* sake and *mine.* Sarah I would sooner come home not worth a cent in the world than have anything befall you or that little one. Sarah about those boots I would rather not have them. I have good government shoes. I dont want you to lay out too much expence when I can get along without it, Keep the money for your self. I am much obliged to you Sarah. For the world sake tell me if you received an allotment draft from me of $13.50. Tell me in the next [letter] without fail for I sent it to you before we went into to Battle. The other Boys sent theirs the same time and all have arrived safe. Now Sarah go to Mothers a spell. Dont you Pay Mr Slight anything. I dont Know what the amount is so let it [go] and if God spares my life to return i will Pay him. For I do not know what the amount is. Sarah God Knows I wish you were in trenton and *I were with you dear.* I was took with my cold the day after jim Havens left. When I told him to tell you to send me that cough syrup I little thought I should need it so quick. My cough is almost cured. I have used up the whole Bottle. I have some Pains in my arms and legs when I exert my self which feels a good deal like Rehumatism but I hope not. Sarah I hope joes folks uses you well. I think they ought to By what your Father told me in a letter the other day that you had been most faithful in your tendance on the children when they were sick. Sarah I am afraid you do to much. You know I told you when I went away that as long as I could support you I did not want you to do anything. But Sarah I know you are not of that dispotion [disposition] to be idle. Well Sarah I must say good By. God Bless you Both are the Prayers of your affec Husband

Corp J. H. Pardington[1]

Direct the same
Kiss for you and that little treasure
Write soon

1. John had been promoted to corporal.

Camp Isibell[1] Near Belle Plain Va
Sunday night Jan 18/63

My dear Wife

I will Pencil a few lines to you in rather a hurry. I am a good deal Better and able to take my Place in the ranks again thank God. We are under marching orders again with sixty rounds of cartridge in our Boxes and three days rations in our Haversacks. In all Probility we shall cross the Rapanack River again but I hope thank God victory will crown our arms this time. I hope they will not allow our army to be butchered again in such away as they did last time. I beleive we start to morrow morning at eight oclock. It will be to bad to leave our Warm houses and to lay again with only them shelter tents to cover us. But anything to Put down this Rebelion. I hope being exposed again wont give me another worse cold. It is very cool weather warm sun shine days with very cold night. God help the Poor wounded soldier that has to lay out all night on the Battle feild for we believe there is a great Battle empending. God only knows what side will conquer. But we believe our Cause is just and right and the old saying is right is might. God Prosper our arms is my Prayer. But I tell you Sarah I dont like much to cross that river in the same Place as we did before. I would not care so much if we only had them on equal footing. But to take them w[h]ere they are behind such entrenchment and Barricade it dont seem fair. But What to be will be I suppose. I suppose the Papers will soon have another victory or a defeat to anounce. Now Sarah I am not agoing to write you much more this time. This is no answer to any of your letters. Only to let you [know] that we are going to move for you told me to always write and tell you when we were going into ———[2] but I am not certin but yet it looks like it now. Give me your Prayer Dear Wife in my behalf and may heavens choicest Blessing rest upon you and that little darlin. Good By. Give my love to Mother and all. A Kiss from your affec Husband and Father

John Pardington

Direct the same
Write soon

1. Camp Isabella, named for Colonel Morrow's wife, who was present during the winter months.
2. John seems to have self-censored his letter in case it got into enemy hands.

monday morning
Near Belle Plain Va
Jan 19/63

Dearest Wife

I have just received you letter dated Jan 11 and 13th and I tell you I was glad to hear from [you] and Baby. It found me enjoying good health again thank God which I hope will find you enjoying good health. Wrote you a letter yesterday. It was no answer only to let you know that we were under marching Orders to leave. I will send it in the same envelope with this so I shall not write you a very long one this time. John Alvord and Henry Hudson has got a commission in the same Reig as Jim Havens.[1] They leive for home to morrow. I wish some one would be kind enough to send me a commission. May be I will have one yet who knows but I suppose I shall have to earn mine By hard fighting. Sarah I shall endeavor to keep out of the Hospetal as long as I can. I am going to send this letter by John Alvord to be left with Willie. About the letters you say you told me twice that you received that draft. I have not received those letters or else I may have overlooked the letter. But I read them over and over again. But I am glad you have received it and that you get cash instead of Orders. I tell you sarah Hank told me about Gibbie being sick down to joes. But dont say anything about it. We expect to Pack up and Be off before night. But I hope not Dear Sarah. I am glad you went to trenton and enjoyed yourself for a few days. The change will do you good no doubt. I have nothing more to say now. But I will write you a longer one By and By. So Good BY Kiss Maria for me and except the same from your affec Husband and father.

John H. Pardington

Write soon
Direct the same

1. Alvord, Hudson, and Havens were "Trenton Boys" from Company B.

dear Sarah

Burnside's Mud March in Virginia, January 21–23, 1863.

Sunday Jan 26/63
Camp Near Belle Plain Va

My dear Wife

This morning I received two letters from you and I tell you they were received with a greatful heart and a welcome hand and read with eagerness and love *for you and baby*. Dear Wife I received that money safe $20.00 dollars. Sarah it shall not be spent in carelessness nor throwed away for nothing that will do me no good. If I do not need it I will send it Back to you. I can tell better in about a week from now. Sarah tell me who told you I was in the Hospital. Dear Sarah thank God I have not been in. I am getting well fast and able to take my Plase in the Ranks again as a soldier of *Uncle Sam*. Sarah I will not say I am cured completely of my cold for I feel it now on my chest sometimes but yet I feel greatful to God that I am so well as I am. Sarah I can fancy your feelings when you heard that I was in the Hospetal. Sarah now tell me dear. Oh do dear. Oh come now for I know it come from the Reigment for I want to find out who send these things. Dont forget to tell me. But enough of this. Sarah you said you felt Bad when you received my letter. For you said in Mother letter I laid all the Blame to you. Sarah you shall never hear it again from my lips or in my letters for *God* knows dear Sarah I *love you* to well to trouble you with reproach or to find fault. Sarah I did not mean anything when I said it to Mother. I thought probily father was mad because we did not let him have it. For I fell [feel] Sarah now that I dont want to have any body angry or mad at me at this time. So Sarah never let it trouble you again my dear. How I would like to Kiss you and little Maria. So Sarah forgive me wont you (I fancy I hear you say yes dear John and [if] you was here I would seal it with a kiss). Sarah it is splendid weather here now. To day I am sitting outside the shanty. Here it is just as warm and as Balmy as our Michigan june Weather. It is very mudy though. We are encamped on a hill which makes it very Pleasent. We started from here last Tuesday to make another attack on the enemy. We had march[ed] about 15 miles [when] it commenced to Rain and of all the mudy roads you ever see why mud street is a side walk to it in its muddy time. Well we had to return and give it up as a bad job and here we are in our good Old shanty again. I will try in my next [letter] to give you an account of our march for we had the most hardships on this last march than we have seen all the time we have been out. I lay in water one whole night last week and never moved till morning. My whole side and hip just as if it was dead By morning. I thought that was Pretty rough after being sick for about 20 days But thank God I am able yet to do my duty. I received a nice letter from Rayner to day. I tell you Sarah it does me good to get a letter from Rayner he talks so good and give me good advice. I think I shall have to disown Maryann for a sister. I think it is cruel of her to treat me so not to write to me. But never mind dear Sarah I have got *two* to write to which are hardly ever out of my mind day or night. Sarah I suppose you would like to know my feelings before I went into Battle. Sarah you can guess them. I thought of you and that little darling for a few minutes then all was forgotten in the excitements of Battle. Sarah I must say good By God Bless you Both. I will give longer in my next letter. This from your affec Husband and Father

J. H. Pardington

Write soon dear
give my love to all

Camp Near Belle Plain. Va.
Saturday Jan 31/63
John Pardington

My dear Wife.

Yesterday I received a nother letter from you. You said you[r] at trenton waiting to know what to do about sending the box. We sent a letter to Mr McIlhiny to send it right off. But we alltered our minds and sent another one this morning and told him not to send it. For we are rather doubtful if we will receive it or not. I hope he will get it in time. Dear Wife I am sorry we said anything about it because no doubt it [h]as caused you a good deal of trouble. But never mind dear if God spare our lives to come home we will repay it in love to the loved ones at home.

Dear Sarah about my health. It is not very good. I can assure you I wrote to you in my last that I was real smart and so I was but as I was afraid it was to good to last. I was took down again Tuesday with the Bloody dysentry. But dear Sarah I have got it checked on me and am now getting better. Sarah I used a dollar or two of that money you sent me. I could not eat the government rations so I had to buy a few delicies [delicacies] such as Biscuts and cheses and a few dried Herrins [herring] and I do not know what I should have done without them.

Dear Sarah I never told you what I wanted that money for. Sarah I thought some of trying with rayners help to get a furlough if I did not get better. I hate to ask you for money Sarah but I thought in a case like that that I would not be ashamed to ask for it. I know dear Sarah you need all you have got By you. But as long as I am well I will not trouble you for any. I shall keep it a few days longer and if I dont need it for that Purpose I will send it most all back.

Dear Sarah you said about going to Rayners to spend a month. Go By all means. But when you start write me a letter before you go. So I can direct your letters to Saginaw. And mind and write when you get there so to tell me if you arrived all right without any accident to you or Baby. Mind and send me your directions when you get there. Sarah if you go see that your things [are] all safe before and if you leave your letters behind let mother keep them for you. Sarah go. It will do you good and I wish you a safe jurney and a *happy time.*

Sarah you would hardly know me now. I dont look like I did a month ago. I am got Pretty thin but I hope I will soon flesh up again.

Now Sarah I must soon come to a close. I have not been [in] the Hospetal. When I do go in do not fear Sarah But what I will tell you of it. I think you and addie had no busisiness to read that letter of Alixs. Tell her we need soldiers and if Alix dont come out he had Better go to *work.* Stop till I come home. Well Sarah good By give my Kind love to mother and except my most sincere love from your John. Kiss Baby for me. I guess she must be some [baby] by what Mr McIlhinny says she is a Beiutiful creature. A Kiss from your affec Husband and Father

John H Pardington

You Know my directions

Dont be surprised By the writing on the envelope it is mine. I have received six letters from you this month which I am well Pleased and will give you a good kissing when I God willing get home

John

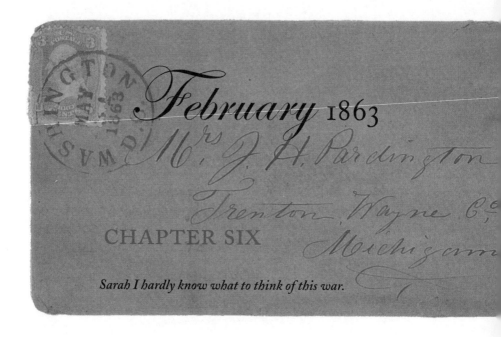

February 1863

Mrs. J. H. Pardington
Trenton, Wayne Co.,
Michigan

CHAPTER SIX

Sarah I hardly know what to think of this war.

Conditions improved immensely under General Hooker. Although weak in some areas, he was a good administrator, and he proceeded to court-martial or dismiss incompetent officers and completely reorganize the suppliers of services. Dishonest quartermasters were no longer overlooked, and the troops were overjoyed to be eating fresh vegetables, fruits, soups, and stews occasionally, instead of the usual hardtack and fried pork. Sick men were getting much better care from the cleaner, newly organized hospitals, and they were able to return to their units. Extremely snowy weather affected camp life. Unable to drill much of the time, the men grew bored, and too much free time led to great homesickness.

Much to John's dismay, someone at home had spread the rumor that he had been killed, upsetting Sarah needlessly. He reassured her that his health was much better and that he had high hopes for General Hooker. John asked Sarah to teach little Maria to say "Father" instead of "Papa," because "it sounds more likely."

February found the men of the Twenty-fourth turning more and more to religion; their spiritual needs were great following the Battle of Fredericksburg. Chaplain William C. Way encouraged his homesick flock with rousing sermons, which John found comforting.

Because of the defeat at Fredericksburg, there was great anti-war sentiment at home. Many young men hesitated to enlist, much to John's disgust and the dismay of the regiment. They were determined to fight to the end.

Headquarters of the Twenty-fourth Michigan at Camp Isabella, Belle Plain, Virginia, during the Winter of 1862–1863. Sketched by H. J. Brown of the Twenty-fourth Michigan.

Camp Near Belle Plain
Feb 4th 1863 Va

My dear Wife

I have just received your loveing and affec letter. Sarah I cant describe my feelings when I read it. To know that there was one, although far away that loved me so dear and true. God Bless the day dear Sarah That I first called you Wife. For Sarah if any woman deserves that sacred title it is *you*. Sarah dear Praise your Baby for I love to hear it Praised. Why shouldent I when you love it so. I am much obliged to you for that Peice of Poetry called the *Soldiers Wife*. I think it Pretty. Now dear Sarah I want to give you a little Peice of advice, now for my sake Keep up your courage and spirits. That['s] what I try and do. For I know it is for your sake. Sarah do not get discouraged and downhearted. My health is getting first rate again, dear Sarah. We have very cold weather here now with considerable snow on the ground. It is snowing now. We have not much news here just now. We are still in our winter quarters which makes it very comfortable for us. I think some of going over to see Elias to-morrow. His Reigment is about six miles from here. If I go I shall stay all night with him. I like him first rate and we both think a good deal of each other. Oh dear Sarah what would I give to see you both. I bleive I would sacrifice my Hand to Clasp you round the neck and imprint one loveing Kiss on those lips that oft times I have Pressed before.

But Keep courage dear for my self. Let us Put our trust in God and all will be well for I think Sarah that he has indeed Blessed us. Dont you think so dear And ought not we to thank him Sarah. I know you say yes. Well How are all Joes folks. Are they well. Sarah I can not Blame you dear for not going there to mother for I Know the house is very cold and you say that mother is going to Rayners to visit. I told you to go in my last letter. But Sarah if you like to wait till I get home (God Willing) we will go together. But Sarah suit yourself dear and you will suit me.

I received Alix letter yesterday and sent and answer to it this morning. He says I have got a smart little girl there. I know she must [be] some [baby] or else the folks would not Praise her *so*. I tell you Sarah I begin to feel *Proud* of her. I must now dear Sarah draw my letter To a close. Ira and Hank are well so are Jim McIlhenny. Good By My dearest. Good By and may God in Heaven Bless you my dearest Wife and daughter. A Kiss for you Both from your affec Husband and Father

John H Pardington

Direct the Same
Give my love to all Write soon

John

Your letter I received was the 28th of Jan. Enclosed I send you a Picture of our shanty I drew of it. It is dug down about two feet in the ground. The four you see there are myself, Jim McIlhinny, Bill Smith and L. Veo[1]

John

this is a true likeness

1. Bill Smith and Lafayette Veo were both "Trenton Boys" in Company B.

My dear Wife

I have just received your Loveing
and affec Letter. Sarah I cant describe my
feelings when I read it. to know that
there was one, although far away
that loved me so dear and true. god
Bless the day. dear Sarah That I first
called you Wife. for for Sarah if any
woman deserves that sacred title it is
you. Sarah dear Praise your Baby for
I love to hear it Praised why shouldent I
when you love it so. I am much obliged
to you for that Peice of Poetry Called
the Soldiers wife. I think it Pretty
Now dear Sarah I want to give you a
little Peice of advice. now for my
sake keep up your courage and spirits
that what I try and do. for I know it
is for your sake. Sarah do not get
discouraged or downhearted. My health
is gitting firstrate again,

dear Sarah

dear Sarah we have very cold weather
here now with considerble snow
on the ground it is snowing now
we have not much news here
just now. we are still in our wint
ers quarters. which make it very
comfertable for us. I think some
of going over to see Elias to morrow
his Regiment is but six miles
from here if I shall stay all
night with him I like him first
rate and we both think a good
deal of each other. Oh dear Sarah
what would I give to see you both
I bleive I would sacrifice my
Hand. to Clasp you round the
neck and imprint one loveing
kiss on those lips that oft
time I have Pressed bfore

But keep courage dear
for my self. let us Put our trust
in god and all will be well

for I think Sarah that he has
indeed Blessed us dont you think,
so. dear. And ought not we to thank
him Sarah I Know you say yes
well. How are all you folks are
they well. Sarah I cannot Blame
you dear for not going there to
mother. for I Know the house
is very cold and you say that
mother is going to Rayners. to
visit. I told you to go in my
last letter But Sarah if you
like to wait till I get home
(God Willing) we will go together
But Sarah suit yourself dear
and you will suit me.
I received Alix letter, yesterday
and sent and answer to it this
morning. he says I have got a ——
smart little girl there. I know she
must some re else the folks would
not Praise her so. I tell you
Sarah I begin to feel Proud of her

Dear Sarah

I must now dear sarah draw
my letter To a close Ira and Hank
ar well so are jim McIlhenny Good
By My dearest good By and may
god in Heaven Bless you my
dearest Wife and daughter
a Kiss for you Both from
Your Affec Husband & Father
        John H Ardington
        Direct the Same
give my love to all
    Write soon
            John
        Your letter I received
    was the 28#th of Jan

Enclosed I send you a Picture
of our shanty I drew off
it is dug down about two feet
in the ground the four you see
there are myself jim McIlhiny and
Bill smith and L bee
this is a true likeness John

Near Belle Plain Va
Feb 13/63

Dear Wife

I have just received your kind and affectinate letter which was received With Pleasure and joy For Sarah I do love to hear from you and Baby for it does me so much good. It make me in such good spirits to hear from my distant But loveing Wife and *daughter.* Well dear so you have a report that I was killed. Well Sarah if Jim Warfeild[1] or any Body else dont Listen to them because you know dear there are some that like to start such *rumors* you know. Well Sarah I am Private no longer. I am the same as Jim Havens was. Two stripes on my arm. So much for tending to duty and *conduct.* Nate Holistead [Nathaniel Halstead] is the same. Well dear Sarah I did not calculate to be Private all my time in the army. If I have got to earn a commisin By hard fighting God give courage and health to do it. Sarah I would like to know what Belinda wants you to take. You said in your last [letter] but one that because you would not take all she says. Is it in regard to me dear. If it is Sarah keep nothing Back from me will you. Tell me all your troubles dear. Dont be afraid. I would sooner have you tell them to me than have you suffer and me not know it. Dear what awful Paper you have down there. Well Sarah there is not much news here now the same as usual. I see Elias the other day. He was well and said he received a letter from you so you must not expect a longer letter from me this time. Gen Hooker[2] is getting the army in good order again and I hope he will for I would like to see Gen Hooker end this war for I think he is the right man in the right Plase and I hope now they will give him a chance. Sarah I hope Mr McIlhenny got our letter in regard to not sending the box. For we alltered our mind for we do not know what minute we may move. For I tell you Jo Hooker is getting the army good. So I suppose we shall soon try the rebels again, well so be it Sarah. I should be ashamed if I was Jim Warfeild and the other Boys around there. Their country in the greatest Peril and every man needed. Sarah I dont believe I could take one of them by the hand with good will. Sarah a young man that will stay at home is a *coward* and ought to be treated as *one*. Perticular a single man. Shame on them I say dont you. Well my dear I must close. It is bed time. Kiss my little darling for me and except one from Your Loveing and affec Husband and father

John Pardington

Direct the same
Good night God Bless you Both is the Prayer of your affec John
Remember me to all
Write soon

1. Probably James Warfield, aged nineteen, listed in the 1860 Census as the son of Henry Warfield of Wyandotte, Michigan.
2. Major General Joseph Hooker took command of the Army of the Potomac upon the retirement of General Burnside.

Camp Near Belle Plain Va
Headquarters 24th Mich Vol
Saturday Feb 21/63

My dear Wife

Last night I received a letter wrote while you was up to your fathers dated Feb 11 and most happy I was to hear from my dear Wife and Child. Sarah I was sorry to hear you was so lonesome. Do dear Sarah keep up good heart and spirits for my sake and the sake of that dear little treasure of ours. Well my Pet I am in the Best of health and Spirits, *thank God.* I never felt better in my life. I received a letter the other day from you about you had sent the Box. We have not received it yet but we expect it every day. But I am rather affraid of the Brandy that is in it. If they enpect [inspect] it in Washington and find the Brandy in it they might confiscate the whole [thing]. They do it sometimes. But I hope we will get it safe. I will write as soon as we get it. You say you would like to be a mouse in one Corner. Of course you would be the *female.* I should like to be the male one in the same *Corner. You Know.* Sarah I witnessed a most revolting spectical this morning.

Six men were tried for desertion while we were marching on the enemy at Fredericksburg. They were tried By Court Martial and sentenced which was carried into effect this morning. I rather think you cant guess what it was. Well I will tell you. First our Bragrade was drawn up in solid square. The Prisners were in the center. They then had their heads shaved and were drumed out before the whole of us and were disgracefully decharged from the service of uncle Sam. One of them was from our Company. His name was James Newington from Wyandotte. So if any of them around there should see him let them Point the finger of scorn at him. Sarah before I would under go the same as they did I would sooner be brought home in my coffin to you as bad as I want to see you dear I never could desert. Sarah I never could Bring such disgrace on you and my little darling. Well Sarah we have not much news here now we are still in our old quarters and likely to stay for awhile to all appearance. For the roads are terrible yet. Day before yesterday we went out on Picket. The whole Brigade and a most terrible time we had. We was out about sixty hours with[out] any sleep. I never see such a snow and rain storm before. All the time we were out all we had with us were our Rubber Blankets. The morning we started there was about 8 inches snow on the ground and in 24 hours you could not see any hardly. I tell you Sarah I never knew before what a man could stand. When we lay down to rest ourselves we had to lay some Rails down to lay on and the water would rin [run] in streams under us. No tents and stand that for sixty hours. You might think this Sarah a hard story but it is the truth. Talk about hardships here is where you will find them. But thank God I dont seem any the worse for it.

Well my dear I hope you will enjoy your visit up to your fathers. I should like to be with you firstrate. If you are up there when you get this give my love to all. To morrow is sunday. I should like to be with you to go to Church. Well good by my dear. Good By and may God in heaven Bless you and that little dear. How I should like to see her Sarah. If you could only know my feelings in regard to you Both. Sometimes I can Hardly contain my self. But I Keep up my spirits for your Sakes. Good By. Remember me to all enquiring friends, and except the love of your affec Husband and father

John H. Pardington

A Kiss to Both
Write soon

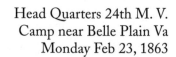

dear Sarah

Sunday Feb 22
Since I wrote this letter last night when I went to bed the
stars was shining Bright. Now there is over 1 foot of snow on
the ground and if it snows till night like it does now there
will [be] 18 inches. It is very cold to. Good By

John

Head Quarters 24th M. V.
Camp near Belle Plain Va
Monday Feb 23, 1863

My dear Wife

I received your kind and affec letter to day Wrote while you was up to
Fletchers. I was glad to hear you and the Baby kept such good health.
Which I am enjoying myself at Present thank God. Well Sarah there is
no news here. The same old drill life when a soldier is in camp. For I tell
you a soldier life is dull when we are doing nothing. For it is such bad
weather here we cant even drill. We have about one foot of snow on the
ground.

Well dear Sarah how I would love to see you and little maria. I dont
hardly blame you for being lonesome. Sometimes for to tell you the truth
dear Sarah I feel so myself at times that I hardly know what to do with
myself. But I hope dear Sarah the time is not far distant when I once
more shall be with my dear Wife and child. But Sarah I hardly know
what to think of this war. But I rather think we are here for our three
years. But I hope not for I should hate to stay here three years and not see
you and Baby. She will be quite a girl wont she if I have [to] stay so long.
But I hope dear Sarah it will not be the case. Do you remember the time
Sarah just after we got married you went up home for a week and I came
for you in the cutter. Well Sarah I thought that week was an awful while

to be from you. The 29 of this month will be six months since I last kissed your lips on the dock in detroit. Sarah will you ever forget that time. I often think of it and think how foolish I was to leave you and sacrifice all the comforts of life besides the company of a loveing Wife and child. But never mind dear Sarah the time I hope will soon come when we shall be again together to enjoy one another company never to Part again till death shall Part us. Sarah will you Please me and learn our little girl to say *father* instead of *Papa*. No offense Sarah only I think it sounds more likely and Better for I always thought Papa was to Babyish when children grow up.

Well Sarah I have not much more to write for I sent a letter to you yesterday. If you had been here yesterday you would have thought there was a big Battle here the way our Batteries fired there guns in Honor of Washington Birthday. I tell you it Put us in mind of Fredericksburg the day it was bombardid. It was an awful stormy day. We have had a tremendious snow storm here about as cold a one as I have seen in Michigan. Ira has been sick with the Direaheria But I believe he is getting Better. Well good By Sarah till the next time. Give my love to all. Kiss mother for me. Tell Father I wrote him a letter over a week ago. Well good By my dear God Bless you. Kiss little Maria for me and except one from your affec Husband and Father

J. H. Pardington
Co. B 24 Mich Infantry
1st Division 1st Army Corp
4th Brigade
Washington D.C.

Is my writing plain enough for you to read tell me in your next [letter]

John

Col Morrows wife and Flanigan wife is here visiting

John to His Wife Sarah

Left August 29 1862
Feb 29 1863
I left you for the Battle feild
Six months ago this day
And who shall speak the Pangs I've felt
Since I first went away

dear Sarah

With dauntless heart we met the foe
Regardless of our life
We rallied fort[h] like valiant men
Amid the awful strife.

O God be merciful to her
Through all these dire alarms
And Bring me safe in Triumph Back
To these dear loveing arms

For she my only hope in life
All others I resign.
I ask no Bliss beyond her love
Sarah. My love for ever thine

John H Pardington To his affec Wife Sarah

I am anxious for thy Presence love
When eve draws on I miss
Thy well known footsteps on the floor
Thy warm and Fervent Kiss
                              John

Death To the Copper Head

"Copperhead" refers to an underground organization dedicated to undermining Union war efforts.

Headquarters 24th Mich Vol

Dear Father

Sarah spoke to me about your helping me to Pay for the house. About turning those colts on the house. Do gest what you think Father to my benefit and your own. I will leave it in your hands to secure the house for me But I dont want Sarah to deny herself and sacrifice to much in being in a hurry to Pay for it. See that she dont and you will much oblige your affec son in law

Corp J. H. Pardington

P.S. I received a letter from you for which I am thankfull. I sent you one the morning before I got it. All send their respects to you and yours

John

To B.F.Knapp[1] In care of S.A.Pardington [written on back of letter]

1. Benjamin Fairchild Knapp, father of Sarah and ten other children, by three wives.

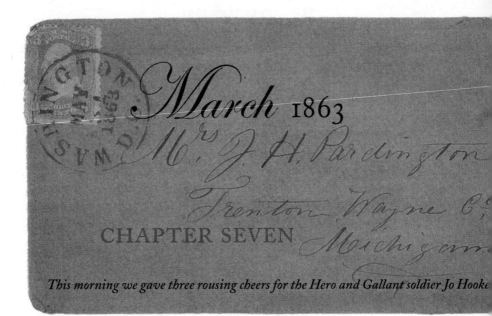

During the month of March, the regiment continued its stay in winter quarters. There was a sense of despondency because of the ongoing anti-war feelings at home. A new party that opposed almost all governmental military measures was formed. Leaders of the new party were encouraging men to desert and others not to enlist. In response, Colonel Morrow, along with other officers, drafted new resolutions. General Meredith asked for voluntary signatures from the Iron Brigade to endorse the following:

> We, the members of the Iron Brigade, do resolve—toilsome as soldiers life may be—that we feel it our duty to carry on this war to the bitter end—and do not desire peace until the last Rebel in arms has vanished from our soil. We warn our friends at home to beware of the traitors in our midst. The blood of thousands of our friends, already sacrificed, cries aloud to you to follow their example. We endorse the Federal Militia Law and hope that the grumblers at home may have an opportunity of shouldering the musket and understanding that no neutrality can exist in the present struggle, and that they must fight, pay, or emigrate.

When the vote was called, the assent was so enthusiastic, the roar of the regiment's cheers so loud, the general and his staff were sent flying from the scene on their rearing and bucking horses.

John's letters home to Sarah and his father were filled with many concerns. He was disgusted to learn that Sarah's brother, William, had deserted, and he asked for the particulars. He reported that they still had not been paid and were due five months' wages. They passed their days drilling and having many inspections while they waited for the roads to dry up. His spirits were low because he was sick once again and they expected a big battle soon.

About mid-month a serious fire destroyed the officers' mess. This created quite a hardship, and when the men discovered their commander's predicament, they competed for the honor of entertaining him and Mrs. Morrow for a meal. The regiment now had a complement of 619 officers and men. Sickness, deaths, desertions, and men taken prisoner at Fredericksburg had taken a heavy toll.

Camp Near Belle Plane
March 2 1863
Monday

Dear Sarah

We have just received the Box. We received it last night. Every thing was in the best Order. What we have tasted is firstrate. It is a splendid Box. I think it is the best that has come to the Reigment. The shirt and things could not suit me better. How shall [I] ever Repay you dear Sarah. Well dear except [accept] of my warmest and tenderest love in repay[ment]. This note is only to let you know that we have received it. We have not tasted any of the Preserves yet but I can judge what they are. I will write more about it in my next. Tell me about your Brother William. I have heard he has deserted. I am sorry to hear it. Write and tell me Perticulars about it. Jim is well. I wish you had been here to see us open it. It was Packed well. Tell willie I am thankfull for the Tobaco he sent. Well my dear good By and may God Bless you are the Prayers of your affec Husband and Father

J. H. Pardington

Answer quick
Kiss Maria for me
P.S. I am enjoying the Best of Health

Jack

dear Sarah

Twenty-fourth Michigan in Bivouac. Sketched by H. J. Brown of the regiment.

Headquarters 24th Mich Vol
Camp Near Belle Plain Va
Saterday night March 6

Dear Sarah

I have just received your letter dated Feb 24th. I was very glad to hear from you. But you did not tell me how our little treasure was. Sarah I love to hear about *her.* Sarah I can always tell when you are away from the Post office for your letters are longer coming than when you are close. I see your letter was dated the 24th but it did not leave Wyandotte till the 28th. You was up to Mandys were you not, *how are the folks there.* I heard about your Brothers desertions. I think he ought to be ashamed of himself. Others are situated just as he is. But I suppose he must see his wife. What kind of a reception would mine give me if i should do the same. (But never) Well Sarah we have received our Box all right and the things tasted firstrate so far. Thank Belinda for me for those Peach Preserves, they are firstrate. Your Fruit cake was bully and so were all the things in generale for which we thank you. When we return we will repay you in *love.* I got a letter from William tonight and he has left Colemans and going to work fathers Plase. Well Sarah we have not got much new here. We are still in our Winters quarters and likely to stay for awhile. But I suppose we will have hot work here before long. Let it come. The quicker the Rebellion will be the sooner Put down. I have not seen Elias for quite awhile. But I beleive he is well. Tell Maryann and Ed I shant trouble them much when I get a furlough. Congress [h]as Passed a law allowing so many out of a hundred to go home on a ferlough for so many days. One out of our company has gone and when he comes Back another can go. To morrow I am going to apply for the next one. I do not know if I will get it or not. If I do not I shall get one after awhile. I hope so for I want to see you very bad and Baby. What do your Father think of Williams conduct. It goes against the grain dont it. Sarah I shall have to risk these letters without stamps. For they are scarce here. Cant you get any w[h]ere you are. I sent a letter the other day without one. I dont like to send them but I cant help it. Well Sarah about that ring. Probily you are right. But I dont remember much about [it]. I thought I gave it to you. Dont you remember the time you would not let me were it (Sarah dont be to free in your conversation about me or anything else at Geore Macdonald. I have my reasons. Keep secret what I have just *wrote*) Well I must say good By. God Bless you and Baby are the Prayers of your affectionate Husband and *Father*

J. H. Pardington

Direct the same

P.S. I thought Sol would turn out that way But Bill Edwards I aint surprised. Write soon

John

Head quarters 24th M.I.
Near Belle Plain, Va
March 11th 1863

Dear Father

Our Reigment has just been drawn up and closed in mass to hear and adopt resolutions to be sent to Michigan. You will no doubt see them in the Papers. The whole 24th Boys officer and Col go in for a vigorious Warfare and not stop till every armed Rebel is swept from the states. I tell you it has got to be done and done it shall be in spite of the copperheads north talk about Peace terms with the traitors. (Pshaw) Give them that *Peace* that knows no Wakeing. By the Bayneot [bayonet] or U.S. union Pill. We go in strong for the draft and conscripting and if there is any resistance just let them send for the gallant Wayne Co. Tigers. We would make them step to a tune they would not very much like. We want them in the feild and have them we must. Every man that can bare a gun ought to come. And they will in spite of all they can do without they Play the run away for Canada. Old Abe will never succomb to the

dear Sarah

theaves and Rebels never. Father there will be Hot times this summer. But let it come. I hope the war will Be Pushed so that 1863 will [see] our Glourious Union all Right.

When we desperced this morning we gave three rousing cheers for the Hero and Gallant soldier Jo Hooker. Well Father if any one asks you what the opinion of the 24th [is] tell them it is for a vigorous Prosecution of the *war*. If it takes every man in the *north*. It is every mans duty that is able Father. The Army of the Patomic was never in Better fighting trim than it is now thanks to Jo Hooker.

Well I must say good By. Give my love to Sarah and all at home and Beleive me your affec son

Corp. J. H. Pardington

Direct the same
Write soon

Camp Near Belle Plain
March 14 1863

Dear Sarah

Enclosed I send you my likeness. They say it is a firstrate [picture] all But my eyes I think they are to small. I hope it will reach you safe and sound. I wont write much of a letter so the letter wont be to heavy. Dear Sarah I am anxiously looking for a letter from you and I get dissapointed every night the mail comes in. I do hope I will get one to night. The last one was dated Feb 24th and I tell you I begin to feel anxious about you. We have not been Paid yet. They owe us four months wages and over and I dont think they will Pay us for two months yet. Sarah I have got that Bad cough on me again so bad that I cant get hardly my rest nights. Sarah the things was bully. I will tell you about them in my next letter because I dont want to make this to Bulky. James McIlheny got his taken at the same time and is going to send it today. We are takeing it at (Parade rest) how we stand on Parade dress. Well good By. God Bless you dear. Kiss my little dear for me. give my respects to all and Beleive me to be for ever your affec Husband and Father

Corp J H Pardington

Direct the same
Directly you receive this write and tell me without delay. There is a kiss on my lips for you.

John

Camp Near Belle Plain, Va
March 23 1863

Dear Sarah

Last night I received your long looked for letter. To morrow would have made one month since I had [heard] from you and Baby. Yesterday I had wrote a letter to Willie to learn what had become of you or what was the matter for no one knows how my mind was racked to no the cause of so long silence. But thank God the letter came at last and of course I shall not send the letter to Willie but if I had not got one last night I should have sent it. Sarah you say you will never make joes Plase your home again, you will work out first. (never) Dear Sarah as long as you are a wife of mine. I will sacrifice Honor and life it self before you shall do it. Sarah if you had seen the Blood rush to my Brow when I read it. What a wife of mine working out with that little darling. Why it almost makes me crazy to think of it. It is well you told me not to write to joes folks, curse them if I must say so. But let it drop. Enclosed I will send you seven dollars. I was keeping it to come home on a furlough but I will give it up now. I should like to see you. For you do not know the anxiety I have for you of late. I was much obliged to you for the news of the Riot at detroit. But I had read it over a week ago. Your letter was almost two week a coming. I guess you dont go to the Post office very often for you say you got three of my letters at once. Well Dear we are still in our old quarters and likely to stay for a week or two yet. But I suppose we will soon have to learn for to fight again. We have about 3 inches of snow on the ground and snowing still. I cant see what has got in to the government why they dont Pay us. They owe us now almost 5 months wages. Sarah if you stand in need of money use that you let your Father have. And never say work out again. Do you suppose dear Sarah I could stay here and to know that you were slaveing your self for other folks. (never) So never say it again if you dont want me to desgrace myself. Sarah about your hair of course you can have it cut. You say about the soldiers wives geting hard names. I guess some of them deserve it Sarah. All I can say about the thing in the Box this time the things were first-rate. The shirts and the other dry goods came usefull for I needed them which I thank you Sarah. I sent you my likeness Last week which I hope you have received safe. I hope the Baby will not get the whooping cough. God Bless her Sarah. I used the remainder of the money. The rest I will send you in this letter so I will give up the idea of a furlough. If the government had Payed us I should not have kept it. Well I must say good By. Give my love to all at home. Give miss longs my best respects. Tell them I would write to them if I knew their direction.Good By. May Heaven Bless you both are the Prayers of your affec Husband and Father

A kiss
J. H. Pardington

Direct the same

Camp Near Belle Plain, Va.
Tuesday March 24th 1863

My *dear* Wife,

Seeing that I cannot sleep I will write you a few lines. The resons I cannot sleep I am suffering from a severe cold which has settled on my lungs again. At nights I cannot sleep on account of coughing. I never suffered with cold so much before in my life. It seems that every little cold I take goes right to my lungs. The last one hung on me about a month. I dont know how long this one will [last]. But I hope not for Sarah dear we are ordered to be ready at a moments notice with six days rations with us. I tell you Sarah we cant go far before we meets the Rebels and ere this reaches you dear Sarah God only knows w[h]ere we will be. There will be a hot time before longs. But dear Sarah God and your Prayers give me strength and courage to Pass through whatever may be my lot. Sarah I sent you my likeness some days Back I hope you have received it dear Sarah. Excuse me But about our little child. Bring her up in the way she should go and when she gets big enough to Run around whatch her. Mind what children she goes with or Plays. Learn her to say father and mother—keep an ever watchful eye on her and if God spare her life that she may grow up a true Christain is the sincere Prayer of her Father. For I know it is the advice of her mother. Sarah you will take no offence of what advice I have said will you dear. For life is uncertain here and if I should fall may I meet you Both in heaven. But dear Sarah I trust God will spare me to return to my dear Wife and child. God Bless you Both. Sarah the sword has got to settle this war and the most rigid campaighn of the war will be this spring and sumner and it will commince before many days. For every preperations is made to get redy at a moments notice. Sarah I have Put a little Pocket in that Blue flannel shirt right By my heart and there you and Baby lays night and day. (that is the locket) the one you sent me last. I keep [it] in the Bible and I carry that in my Breast Pocket. So you see dear I have you By me all the time and through every danger. But I will try and not get you hurt.

Sarah I must now close and try and get a little sleep for it is getting late. Dear this is no answer to any of your letter But I was feeling kind of lowspirited so I thought the best medicine would be to write to my dear Wife. Sarah no one knows where we are going when we move but it is strongly hinted that we will try Fredrickburg again. God Prosper and give victory to our arms this time if we do try it again but I almost fear the result. Well dear I must say good night and may God Bless and Protect you Both are the Prayers of your affectinate Husband and Father

John Pardington

Direct the same
Kiss Baby for me and except one for yourself

John

Write soon give my respects to all

Near Belle Plain Va
Headquarters 24th M. I.

Dear Father

I thought I would write you a few lines and wishing you to write and tell me the Perticular about William Knapp desertion for that is the report here amongst his friends in the Reig. But I hope it is not so. But I thought [h]is Patriotism would soon die out. It dont last long in the army. But I hope to God he has not desgraced himself and family. Father as bad as I want to see my Wife and child I do not think I shall ever desgrace them or you as a son in law. Now Father mind and tell me. Well Father we have received our Box all right and Oh the good things did taste so good. Every mouthful I would eat I would think of Sarah. Oh Father How I would love to see her and that little darling but I suppose I must wait Patiently and hope for the Best. But I tell you it tries a man to be away from those we love and swore to cherish and Protect. But as long as I know she is not suffering my spirits keeps up good. But if I knew she was suffering nothing on earth would keep me from her. Even if I had to dishonor my self. But God *Forbid* that. Come Father you are behind hand with that letter I am looking anxiously for it. Ira has got his box all right. I tell you we love how it puts us in mind of home. Well Father what is your oppinion on the war. When do you think it will end and so forth. Mine is I think we will have to stay our three years out. What do you think of it. Tell the young men around there they had better come now as last for we will want more. Tell them to look out for the *draft* it is comeing slow But sure. We have got a foe to deal with that no nation ever had before. They will fight us to the *death*. Well they have Promoted me to Corporal. Ey so much for tending to duty. I tell you what it is Father. If I have got to stay three years and God spares my life I want to come out and weare something on my *shoulders*. Because if a soldier tends to his duty there is no need of him being Private all [h]is term is there. Well good By. Kiss Sarah and the little one for me and give my love to all at home and respects to all enquiring friends. I Remain your Dear Son

J. H. Pardington

Direct the same

Headquarters 24th Mich Vol. Va.
March 26 1863

Dear Sarah

I have just receved a letter from you to night which I was thankful to hear that you were both well. Sarah I am realy sorry to hear you have got a boil on so *tender a spot*. Sarah excuse me for drawing a line under But to tell you the truth I could not help smileing when I read it. Although I was sorry and I hope ere this reaches you that it will be well. Sarah I have sold a revolver to Willie. He will hand you the five dollars. I would not have sold it to any body else so cheap But Willie being a good fellow why I let him have it. I gave twelve shillings for it so I will make three dollars and a half on it. That wont be bad. But the revolver is worth 10 dollars. Sarah we expect to be Paid soon. I hope so for they Probly Pay us 4 months Pays. If they do I can send you 40 dollars for I know you kneed it. Well Sarah there is not much news here now. We expect to march every day. Sarah you wanted to know about the little bit of mystery as you call it. The reason is Sarah if I must tell you there is something about Hank that I dont like. I think they are the kinds of folks to get up suspission. I may be wrong But I dont want anything said there concerning me. Sarah not as I think concerning you (God forbid). Sarah forgive me if it does not meet your approbation. I have my suspicion about them and I cant help not as I meen about your visiting there. I have nothing against that. Go there all you like. But in conversation dont give them any enformation conserning me. More I can tell when I get home. But enough of that. Sarah I dont think I shall be able to come home this spring or sumner. Next Winter if my life is spared *I must see you at all hasards*. I know it will be a dissapointment to you for dear Sarah it is a great one for me, God Bless and Keep you Both in health are the Prayers of your John. Sarah have you received my likeness yet. Jim McIlhinny folks has got his and we both sent the same time. Give my love to all. Kiss mother for me when you see her. God Keep her in health and in life for Sarah how should I feel if she were taken away and me not see her. God Bless her. Give my love to her. Sarah good night and may heaven choiest

Blessing rest upon the head of you and our little treasure are the Prayers of your affec Husband and Father

Corp J. H. Pardington

Direct the same
Write soon
A kiss for Both

Near Belle Plain, Va
March 30, 1863

Kiss our little treasure for me
Remember me to Mr Jones folks
Dear Sarah

I received your letter last night dated 22nd in which you said you had received my likeness in which I am glad to hear. You said you kissed it but it did not kiss you back again. I wish I had been in the case. I would have kissed you good. Dear Sarah you[r] letter was a beautiful letter so affectinate just like you. Oh how I long to see you. My heart yearns toward you and our little dear. What a large girl she will be if I should have to stay 2 or 3 years wont she. I hope she will know me when I get Back. How I should feel for her not to notice me. But under your care dear Sarah I have no fears of that.

Sarah you said again that you were not going to make Joes your home again. You said that Mrs McIlhiny thought you would be more contented in trenton. Sarah would you. You asked me to write to your father. I think there is no need of that. Dear Sarah if you think you are in the way anywhere look you out a room or a house in trenton and go there and live. But mind Sarah if you do go there get a respectible one in a respectible Part of the vilage. Sarah I dont think of any Plase in trenton you must Pick for yourself. Write and tell me as soon as you get one. But now Sarah I have a word to say to you. If you go in trenton which you can with my free will. If you need money I want you to draw on that money you let your father have. I dont want it said that a wife of mine wanted any thing when there was money at her command. Now dont forget what I have just told you. That money is yours dear Sarah use it with Pleasure. (if God spares my life and two hands I can earn a living) for you know dear Sarah our Pay here in the army is very uncertain. They owe us now five months wages and we dont know when we will get Paid. That is the Reason why I want you to use that money. For I want you and baby to look well in trenton this sumner. Dear Sarah now I shall get some Papers from you shant I. Now dear write as soon as you move, move as soon as

dear Sarah

it suits you. You have my free and hearty consent and may happiness attend you. Sarah that was a splendid letter you wrote me. It made me feel so good and happy. Sarah my honest opinion is that the rebelion will be ended this sumner. My cough is not much Better. Sarah will you send me a bottle of that cough syrup again. That is the only thing that eases me. I must now close with kind love to all and except the same from your affec Husband and Father

J. H. Pardington

Direct the same
A kiss for Both
Write soon.
Sarah tell me what was the matter at Joes. Now dont forget.

John

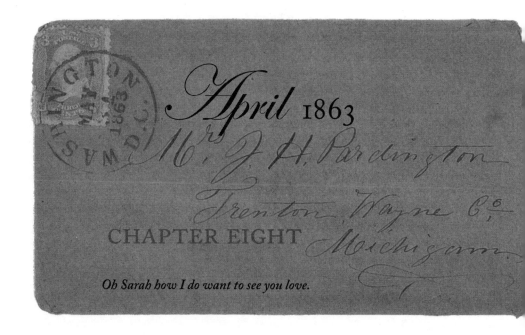

Spring weather had arrived in Virginia. Although John described it as "splendid," it gave him "a real touch of the Blues for a day or two." He described General Hooker's review of the First Division:

> Dear Sarah yesterday was a grand day for us. That is our Division numbering about 12000 men. We were reviewed by Gen Hooker. I wish you had seen the sight. It was splendid. The men all dressed in their Best with their guns shining Bright and music Playing. It was a sight that would enflame the heart of any Patriot and make [h]is bosom swell with emotion. I tell you Sarah our flag must and shall triumph.

General Hooker was very impressed with the Twenty-fourth. A few days after the review, Colonel Morrow, leader of the regiment, and other officers of the Twenty-fourth were presented to President Lincoln and General Hooker. The general singled out Colonel Morrow with this comment: "Oh, we are old friends. I noticed your regiment the other day; ITS AS FINE AS SILK." The men of the regiment were thrilled to receive such praise, and well deserved it was.

By mid-month they were very close to the enemy. A relatively minor encounter occurred at Port Royal around April 22; they captured horses, mules, and prisoners, but there were no losses in the regiment. There was another encounter at the end of the month at Fitzhugh's Crossing. Asa Brindle, a comrade of John's in Company B, was killed.

Volunteers from the Twenty-fourth Michigan and Fourteenth Brooklyn Crossing the Rappahannock at Port Royal. Sketched by H. J. Brown of the Twenty-fourth Michigan.

The men of the regiment received their first pay in four months, so John could send $36 to Sarah. They were warned by the colonel to send their drafts home with the Rev. William C. Way, chaplain of the Twenty-fourth, as it was not safe to send mail by way of Washington.

The great Battle of Chancellorsville was but a few days away, and the men were ready for it.

Camp Near Belle Plain Va
April 3 1863
Direct the same

Dear Sarah

Last night I received your letter datted March 25th and Hasten to answer I was much Pleased to hear from you and Baby. You said I wish I was there to go to mothers with you and help carry the Baby. *Sarah I wish I was there.* I would carry the Baby all the way. Sarah I got a letter from your father the other day and I answered right off. He write a good letter. Sarah you never mention about Coltrens folks. Where are they. Are they to your fathers yet and what are they doing. It is splendid spring weather here now and it make me more lonesome. Oh I wish I was with you Sarah. Sometimes I get a real touch of the Blues for a day or two then I think well it is no use to give up so I get my spirits again but I cant help it sometimes. Dear Sarah yesterday was a grand day for us. That is our Division nombering about 12000 men. We were reveiwed by Gen Hooker. I wish you had seen the sight. It was splendid. The men all dressed in their Best with there guns shining Bright and music Playing. It was a sight that would enflame the heart of any Patriot and make [h]is bosom swell with emotion. I tell you Sarah our flag must and shall triumph. Well Sarah what ever is Wm going to do in Canada with his wife and family to live on 30 cts a cord. They never can do it as your father said time will show. Since I wrote you last Elias was over here to see me. He was awful mad about Wm derserting. He says he wont speak to him when he gets home. Say Sarah I should not wonder if he should bring you a sister home. I guess she is a Pretty new girl by what he says and I know she is affectinate for I have read some of her letters and they are full of love just like yours. Well Sarah there is not much news here now. We expect every day to leave. Sarah all I ask is my health to stand the Hardships. We will have to go through this summer for we expect some hard times. Well my dear I must draw to a close with kind love to all. Kiss the Baby for me and except the same from Your Affec Husband

J. H. Pardington

Write soon
Ira Flecher is well
I will write a longer letter next time

Camp Near Belle Plain Va
Headquarters 24th Mich Vol
April 5 1863

Dear Sister (Maria can you send me a stamp when you write for they are scarece)

To night I received your long looked for letter. What joy I expeirence when I read it. It made me feel that I had indeed my sister Maria left. Oh Maria do write to me. Well Maria I am a good deal Better of my cough than I was although it has not all left me. Yet I am better. I got a letter from Sarah tonight. I will tell her that I have received one from you and I can fancy how happy she will be to hear of it. Now Maria I want you when you write again to send me one of those Pictures. Never mind if it dont look good. Ill know who it is. I want to see you so bad. Now do send it dear wont you. Tell Dick I shall be very glad to hear from him next time.

Well Maria about a soldiers life it is anything But Pleasent although I am cheerfull. I tell you Maria if I was single I would not care abit. But I tell you my thoughts are of that (*dear Wife and child God Bless them*). I suppose you heard that we were in the battle of Fredricburgs. I tell you it was a Hot Place. Pity we had not gained a victory. But I hope to God next time we will Pay them Back in their own coin. Well Maria a soldiers life is a hard one. A man do not know what he has to Pass through and it is well he dont for I am afraid if he did they would not have many soldiers. Maria tell Dick if he is drafted if he can get a substitute to get one. If he was single I would not talk so but Dear sister it is for your sake for I know how dear Sarah suffers in my absence. Well Maria we expect soon to be marching on the Rebels again and I think under fighting Jo Hooker. Our glorious stars and stripes will soon float over Rebeldom with victory on every *star*. Stars for our friends *stripes* for our foes. Maria I am glad to hear you and Dick are living so Happy and contented together. I wish you much joy. Maria I never thought a man could have such strange feelings before he went into Battle. For the first ten minutes he think of those that are near and dear to him then all is forgetting in the excitement of Battle and the awful sights that meets [h]is eyes. I had two very narrow escapes. One was a common Ball. I heard it coming. I fell down on my face and [it] struck just about two feet from [me] throughing the dirt all over me. The next was a shell that Bursted. It struck down my file leader. Killed or wounded two or three alongside of me. I thought that was a rather close call for the first time But thank God I came out safe. In the second days fight our Company were detailed as scirmishers. That was fun. Woe be to the man that should [showed] his head. I tried my best that day to give a *Grayback*[1] one of Uncle Sams leaden Pills. Well Maria there is not much news here at Present. I hope i will have more to write next time. Now you must give my love to Hellen, Alf, Bob and all my friends and dont forget Dicks (All Aboard). Maria they say mine is such a Beautiful Baby. Only think near ten months old and can creep around. Now good By Maria may God Bless you Both are the Prayers of your affec Brother

J. H. Pardington
Co. B 24th Mich Vol
1st Division 1st Army Corp
4th Brigade
Washington D.C.

Write soon

1. Slang expression for Confederate soldier.

Camp Near Belle Plane Va
Sunday April 5 1863

Dear Sarah

I received your Welcome letter last night and was glad to hear from you But sorry to hear the Baby had the Whooping cough. I hope ere this reaches you that she will be better. Dear Sarah I think they are making soldiers Pretty fast down there.[1] I should think if I was Bill I should hold on for awhile. He will be as Bad as Father was.[2] Sarah I told you in the other letter what to do. To live in trenton get a room or a house up somewhere By McIlhiny. Dont get it in the other Part of town. I dont want you to stay any where dear where you are not wanting [wanted] by no means. I have to much Pride for that.

Well Sarah this is most curious country you ever see. Now the other day it was most splendid Weather you ever see. It would make you sweat just walking and now to day winter is here with all its rigor. The ground is covered with snow and very cold and maybe to morrow it will be warm as june. Sarah if I get a letter from Jo I will send it to you. But I would like to have the full Perticulars about it. Probily Jo will tell me but I should like to have your report about it. I am sorry that anything should have occured. If I had known it I should never have left you there. Now Sarah let me give you a little Bit of advice. When you get in trenton, the Vanhorns have used you Bad. Now have nothing to do with them after you move. None of the family. (mind now) your Father will let you have goody with you and you can get along without *their help*. You know Sarah when you get there they will be good as Pie to you then. Now have nothing to do with them. Sarah you may think me Pretty hard but it is the only thing that will repay them. Visit up around your fathers as much as you like But not on the (South road). You must not forget mother. I am sorry to hear that Father is in such away again. I dont think he will last long. You said about Bill being away from his wife two weeks. That so Sarah how would he stand being away 7 months. I have stood it soo long well enough I get up mornings rather *stiff*. How is it with you *dear*. I think I could make a young soldier without much work or sweating. But then if our lives or [are] spared we must make up for lost time. *Eh Sarah I guess so*. Well enough of that. I must say good By. Remember [me] to Joes folks and to my friends. Kiss the Baby for me and except my warmest love from your affec Husband and father

J. H. Pardington

Direct the same

dear Sarah

Your letter was dated March the 30th Sarah you write well dear

John

1. Refers to increased birth rate at home.
2. Sarah's father had eleven children.

Camp Near Belle Plain Va
Sunday night April 5/63

Dear Sarah

I have just received another letter. I am not going to write a long one now for I wrote you a long one this morning and sent it off. Sarah you spoke to me you could get half of that house of Kittles. Get it as soon as you can for I dont want you to stay at Joes another day longer than you can help. By what I have heard and Sarah what I have told you in another letter when ever you needed money use that you let your Father have. It is yours not mine so use it dear when ever you want it for I want you to look well this summer for it is uncertian when we will get Paid. I hope before long. Sarah I am better By a good deal (thank God).

Sarah you spoke to me about uniteing yourself to the church. Dear Sarah you have my free will and may God help you to live a Christian. Sarah I love you as I never loved before. God Hasten the day that I shall once more clasp you to my beating heart where your Pictures lay to night. Well dear I got a letter from Maria tonight and such a nice one and she is going to write to me once a week and send me her Picture. Wont that be good dear. Now Sarah go to trenton and get settled as quick as you can. It shall *never* be said that we depended on them. That is Joes folks for a home never. Now dear don't deprive yourself of anything for if God spares me to come home whole I can earn a living again. So good night my dear. It is getting late and I must to Bed (Oh dear). Kiss little Maria for me and except one for yourself from your affec Husband

John H. Pardington

Write when you get settled
Direct the same

Headquarters 24th M. V.
Near Belle Plain Va
April 8 1863

Dear Sarah

Your letter of the 2nd came duly to hand and [I] can truly say it was joyiously received I am ambslt [absolutely] cured of my cough and I hope

I will not have a nother attack of it this spring. Gen Hooker gave our Reigh [Regiment] quite a High compliment the other [day] after he had reveiwed us. He said it was the finest looking Reigment the most soldiering and neatest in the army of the Patomic. He told it Persinal to our Col and other officers standing around. I tell you Sarah that is a great feather in the caps of the Boys of the 24th and comeing from the lips of our Great Commander in chief of so vast an army. Well Sarah there is no news of importance here at Present. I hope ere this letter reaches you you will [be] nicely settled in Trenton and alone. Mind and have goody with you for I should not like to have you there alone. Because I would not have you to Joes any longer. You say there is things there done there that tries you. I dont doubt you a bit Dear Sarah. It as you say if we had known as much as we do now you had better believe I would not have sent you there on any account. But as you say peraphs it is all for the Best. I should think it would turn father crasy to have so many children there. Oh no dear Sarah I would do no harm if [I] came on a furlough. *I would be very careful* but I guess we would Both be so loveing that we would forget our failings. (Eh) I would risk it wouldent you Dear. Oh how [I] long to see you and dear Babys face. Of *course* I do not want to see anything else of you. *Oh no just try me on (All Aboard).* Well enough of that dear Sarah. I wonder what is the matter with rayner. He dont write now. I have wrote him to or three letters But he has not answered them. Sarah I have often thought if our Parting wont be all for the Best you know how I used to use you sometimes stoping out nights and so on. Well Dear when it came into my head to enlist I dont think no soul on hearth [earth] could have stop me. It seem that if I was to leave you to amend my ways and thank God dear Sarah if he spares my life to return to you it shall be amended in constant love and care of you. Dear I never told you this before but I think so my self. Well Sarah I must come to a close. Give my kind regards to all. Kiss my little treasure for me and except one warm and loveing kiss from your affec Husband and Father

John H. Pardington

Direct the same

good by my love good by

Write soon Dear

How would you like to have your letters directed like this all the time Mrs John H. Pardington

dear Sarah

Dear Sarah

It is such a beautiful day which make me very lonesome so I think the only way to cure it will be to write you a few lines to let you know that I am enjoying Bully Health again thank God. Which my dear I hope these few lines will find you and Baby enjoying the same blessing.

Sarah My dear I hope ere this reches you, you will be comfortable situated in trenton. Now mind you send me a Paper once in a while wont you. Send me a Paper that as got some good stories in [it]. Willie will get you some. Send me a Harpers Weekly now and then. Our Chaplin Preached us a very nice sermen to day which made a good many think of home and those we love *so dear*. Oh Sarah how I do want to see you love. I can hardly contain my self sometimes. But my dear let us hope for the best. I hope it wont be to long before I shall feel those dear arms around my neck and that warm and loveing kiss. Kiss baby good for me. I am expecting a letter from you to night I hope I wont be disapointed. How are all the folks. How is Mrs Clee Health. Has she been eating *Dried apples*. I guess Johnny has been generious. Well Sarah I shant write many more lines for I may get one from you to night or tomorrow and then I shall have to write again. There is not much news. Ira and Hank are well and Jimmy McIlhiny Hollstead and the rest. I was rather surprised to hear that Hanks girl was married. Absence conquered love with her. But it dont with us does it dear. I know you will say (no Siree). Well good By My dear Wife and may Heaven choisest Blessing rest upon you Both are the Prayers of your affec Husband and Father

John H. Pardington
Co. B 24th Mich Infantry
1st Division 1st Army Corp
4th Brigade
Washington D.C.

Write soon
Write soon

Camp Near Belle Plain Vergenia April 14th 1863
Dear Sarah

I received a letter from you last night and one to night. I will answer them both together. The one I got last night was the one that had the Pattern of your Dress in [it]. I like it firstrate. I think it is firstrate and Pretty. The letter I got to night was dated April 7th. It was a splendid letter full of love and affection. A letter worthy from a true *Wife* and loveing *woman*. Dear Sarah I love you as I never loved before. God Grant the time when we shall meet again in warm *Embrace*. Sarah you say truly if Belinda was Placed as you were she would not act so. That is so dear. Sarah there is no knowing what time will tell. She may be Placed as you are. God help her if ever she is. Well Sarah I long to get a letter and to hear that you are comfortable Placed in trenton. Get that house of Kettles By all means for you wont have to run to the river for water. Yes dear Sarah I can read your letters firstrate. I have no troble at all in reading them. You improve greatly Dear. *Although you are green from the Country.* Dear Sarah do you know when I red that in your letter, when you must excuse your Writing for you was green from the country. Yes dear Sarah I do remember it and a shade of shame Passed over my face when I read it and when I thought of days Past and gone. But all that is forgiven aint it dear. Sarah I know you will say yes. Well Sarah when I red your letter I had a great notion to sit down and write to Belinda but then again I reccolected you told me not to write to them. And I wont But it would do me a good deal of good to write them a good but Harsh letter. But for your sake I wont. Well Sarah we are making great preperations to move. We expect to move this week at the furthest. We have got to cross the Rapahanock again but I guess not in the same Place some miles above freerickburg. I hope we wont get drove back this time. Sarah I will try and write you a letter when we go in to Battle for we cant march two days before we are up to the enemys. I tell you Sarah we aint no further from the Rebels than is our camp that from Detroit to trenton. We can go that in one day. So I tell you we aint got to go far before we meet them. The day we move onward I will try and send you a note to let you know. Pray for me Sarah that God will take care of me through all danger and harm and Bring me safe to my wife and *child*.

[rest of letter is missing]

dear Sarah

Dear Wife

Last night I received that Bottle of medicene for which in return except of a loveing [Kiss]. Well dear Sarah I think this will be the last letter I shall be able to write to you before we move for we are all ready. Only waiting for Old Joe [Gen. Hooker] to say the word. Dear Sarah I received a letter from Willie in which he said that you were going to move in to Kittle house. I am glad to hear it. Now dear Sarah I dont want you to sacrifice yourself on close [clothes] for I want you to look and appear good in trenton this summer. For no doubt you will attend _church_ strictly. Oh how I wish I was there to go with you dear Wife and Baby. God Bless you are the Prayers of your John. Sarah I am not going to write a long letter now for I expect a letter from you to night and then I shall have to write again. This is only to tell you that I have received that Bottle of Syrup. So good By my dear. God Bless you Both. Kiss little Treasure for me and ever think me your True and affec Husband and Father

J. H. Pardington

Direct the same

P.S. What do you think. We have eight day raition to carry on our Backs besides our other things. Quite a load aint [it] dear. My cough is better almost well.

Thank God

Your John

Camp Near Belle Plane Va
April 18 1863

Dear Wife

To night I received your welcome letter and was glad to hear you were settled in trenton. I know dear Sarah all you want to make you contented is you[r] _John_ then I guess you would be all right. I should think Mrs Plumb[1] will be firstrate company for you. O how I would like to be with you to night. I guess we would _hug_ and talk some before we went to sleep wouldent we _dear_. Well dear Sarah I did not think I should be here in this _camp_ to write you another letter but such is the case. But we are all ready to start dear and then for Hardships and Perils and Privations. But I dont care how much we suffer if we only gain a victory. Sarah I would Willingly lose my left Hand if we whip them out this summer. But I hope and trust God I shall come out all sound. It is splendid weather here now and hope it will continue so. Hank McD is very sick I do not [know] what is the case.

So Addie is running on to Breahers again. I thought she wouldent hold out much longer. Alix then has taken my advice for *soldiers*. That is all right. I am afraid we shall need them. Tell Mrs McIlhiny that Jim is well. Tell Willie that nate Hallstead received a letter from him to night. Tell Mr Plumb I will wright as soon as I can. Now Sarah I hope you will spend a Pleasent summer in trenton as you can. I am so glad you are away from Joes folks. I dont want you Sarah to encouage any of their children to come and stay with [you]. Dont have Sarah [I believe one of Joes children] to come and go to school on any acount will you. Goody will be enough for you when he comes. I shall write your father a letter before long. Oh dear Sarah I love you and I am glad I have got such a good wife and wont I repay this long absence up in love for you and our little daughter. God Bless you Both are the Prayers of your affec and Faithful Husband and Father

J. H. Pardington

Direct the same

Good by my love good by. A Kiss for Both. Remember me to all. Kiss mother for me when you see her.

Dear I am Perfectly satisfied with what you have done. Rest contented. May heaven Bless you

1. Probably Harriet Plumb, aged nineteen, wife of Alford Plumb of Trenton (1860 Census).

Head Quarters 24th Michigan Volenteers
April 20/63
Camp Near Belle Plain Va

My dear Sister Maria

To night I received your most welcome letter and most happy to hear from you and Dick. Maria I received your Picture safe and it did look so natural. Oh I did wish it was the original so I could give you a good kissing. Maria you wanted to know how we killed time in the army. Well we Play Ball and most of the time we drill and then we have enspection and reveius. So you see Maria we have enough to Pass time and then we are on Pickett every now and then. We go for three days at a time. Then you know that is a change from the dull life of camp. Maria you often thought how we sleep. Well I will tell you. It is now allmost eight months since we left *Detroit* and I have not slept with my *Pants* off the whole

[time] and hardly my coat and sometimes my cartridge Box and Belt. When you are sleeping warm and cosy in your Beds most likely we are on the ground with nothing But our Blankets to cover us. After the Battle of Fredrickburg right after the Battle Our Reigment was on Pickett on the River side. We were on one side and the Rebels on the Other. We dare not have any fire and I did think I should Perish from cold. We had nothing But our Rubber Blankets. It was a terrible cold night. That is where I think I caught my cold for when we moved into this camp I was taken down so I did not do any duty for 20 or 30 days.

Well Maria you wantd to know who of my folks have wrote. They have all wrote to me But Mary ann, Eliza, and Kate. I tell you Maria if I get a furlough this summer I shall not go and see Maryann. She may come [to] me but not me [to] her. For I think she has behaved most shamefull. I have wrote her two letter. Maria if I get a letter from her I dont think I shall answer it. My Brothers write Pretty regular which I shall always remember. I hope to gracious they will draft Ed Button for he [is] nothing but a coward. Do you know maria that he ran away for a week before I enlisted. He did and I have never thought much of him since. Maria a man that will run [away from] his country deserves the death of the *Gallows*. I would willing[ly] Pull the rope if it was my own Brother. I know dick will never run [away from] his country for he will stand a draft first and get out the Best way he can. But I hope for your sake he wont Be. Well Maria I am glad you have got a couple of Quails for Pets and rest assured dear Sister if I get a furlough this summer I will stop and see you going through and comeing Back. Maria we have not been Paid yet. When we are I will get my Picture taken in full uniform gun and all and send it to you. It is only a dollar. I will have it taken at a Parade Rest that way looks the Best. Maria your likness shall do through all the hardships and Battles that I go into, so I shall have you and Sarah with me all the time my two *Best Pets*. I have got you Both in my Bible and carry you in my Breast Pocket of my dress coat. We started to march this morning but the orders were countermanded so we returned Back to our old camp. We had eight days rations on our Back. What do you think maria of a soldier carrying eight days grub on our Back Besides our tent Blankets shirts Ruber Blankets and our gun and sixty rounds of cartridges. Quite a load Maria. (Eh) Well Maria you wanted to know What were the Boys names from trenton. Well there is Nate Hallstead, J. McIlhiny, Wm Smith, Lafaette Veo, John Alvord, H. Hudson, J. Havens, the three last are gone home. O yes there is a nother Er Cady. So you see there is quite a number of trenton Boys together. Well Maria I must close. Give my love to Dick, Alf, Bob and Hellen and all my Friends in Toledo. So good By my dear Sister May Heaven Bless you Both are the Prayers of your affec Brother

> Corp J. H. Pardington
> Co. B 24 Mich Volenteer
> 1st Division 1st Army Corps.
> 4th Brigade
> Washington D.C.

Write soon
A Kiss

> Camp Near Belle Plane Va
> April 28/63

Dear Sarah

Enclosed you find a draft of 36 dollars. You can send me 12 dollars of it so I can come home after awhile on furlough. I must close for we are all excitement here for moving. There is heavy fireing on our right this morning. So good By God Bless you Both are the Prayers of your affec Husband and Father

> J. H. Pardington

Write soon
Direct the same
A kiss for Both

> Headquarters 24th Mich Vol April 28/63

Dear Wife

I received two letters from you and should have answered them before but we have been on a recognasence. That is our Reigment and the 14th Brooklin. We accomplished what we went after captureing a lot of horses and mules [and] Prisiners without the loss of a man. We crossed the Raphannock at Port Royal. We took them By surprise and before they could Bring a foarce large enough to Bring against us we were safe across the River. You will see the account of it in the Paper. You will then see all Perticulars. Mind and send me the Paper for I want to see how they will Praise us. Sarah dear I have got a draft of $36.00 dollars. We got Paid four months wages. But the Col told us this morning that it was not safe to send it By mail from here to Washington. He says that the Chaplin thinks of going to Washington to carry our money and to mail it from there. I was going to send it this morning. But to be safe I will wait till the chaplin goes. Dont you think it will be best Dear Sarah.

dear Sarah

Now Sarah I am enjoying the Best kind of health Thank God. How is our little darlin. Is she well. I did not tell you that Maria sent me her Picture did I. So you see I have got my three Pets with me. Sarah when you receive that draft the Captain has Promised me a furlough. Now if you think dear Sarah that we can afford it send me ten dollars of it. I have got 7 dollars with [me] and the ten you send me will be enough to Bring me home. You know Sarah how we both want to see one nother dont you. Now mind and tell me in your next letter. Sarah I wish I was with you to take your Part against Mrs Kittle and Mrs Plumb. I would make them retreat or else flank them so they would have to surrender. Tell Mrs Kittle I dont think the last name on that list of young soldiers is correct or else I am mistaken. I dont think she has got enough in her to help Johny to make one. But I think if she had one of us soldiers to make one for her I should more likely to beleive for we have got some *laid By Ready for use.* I think when I get home you will have to Put a *curb Bit on me* but then I will be *easy.* Sarah you can act your own Pleasure about Paying ahead for the house. I think you had better secure it. I received a letter from James Havens last night. Sarah it will be quite a while before I can get a furlough but then I shall before long if my life is spared because they are to continue right along. So rest assured dear Wife that I shall see you this summer if God spares my life. Well Sarah I must Bring my letter to a close. I will write again before long for I owe you a letter. But we have had so much to do last week that we have had hardly time to write so I know you will forgive me wont you dear. I will Pay up for it when I get home. Give my love to mother and all my friends Mrs McIlhiny, Addie Alix and all. Jim is well. Good By my dear Wife and child. May heavens choiset Blessing rest on you Both are the Prayers of your affec Husband and Father

J. H. Pardington

Write soon. We expect soon to have enough to do.

John

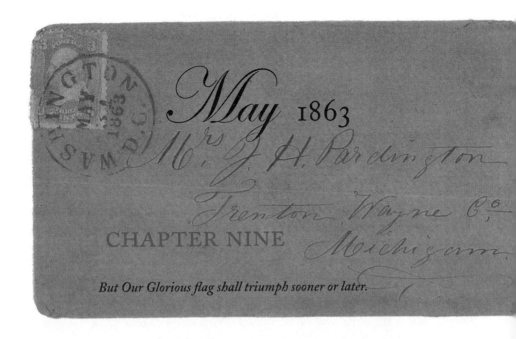

CHAPTER NINE

But Our Glorious flag shall triumph sooner or later.

The Battle of Chancellorsville raged during the first days of May, and Union and Confederate forces alike suffered great losses. The famous Confederate general "Stonewall" Jackson was accidentally shot and killed by one of his own men.

John told Sarah that they had been "fighting and working" for eight days with almost no sleep. He described how their regiment was the first to cross the Rappahannock River in open boats and how they stormed the enemy rifle pits and captured two hundred "Rebs." He felt that they lost the fight because of "the 9 months men and two years men . . . they Break and Run." With their time so nearly finished, they couldn't give it their all.

After the battle, John once again became ill with "the Remittant fever." From a camp near White Oak Church, he told Sarah how very homesick he was, and he described the scene he visualized in his fantasies about returning home. Recovering from his illness, John once again joined his unit.

Camp Way, named for their chaplain, was located in a beautiful area of Virginia on what used to be part of George Washington's family's farm. While on picket duty, John wrote to Sarah describing the area's loveliness, and how it was rather dull as all they had to do was watch the "Grey Backs." They did not fire on one another because, as John said, "it only seems like murder and it dont do any good to either side."

dear Sarah

The end of the month brought a visit from Governor Blair and his wife. A dress parade was held to hear the governor's speech, and General Reynolds reviewed the First Corps. The month's end also saw the reduction of the Iron Brigade from 16,000 to 9,000 men. The terms of the two-years' men and the nine-months' men had expired.

May 1 1863
Battle feild[1]

Dear Wife

I am well and God has spared my life so far. We have been at it three days I think we will be succesfull. We have lost some in our reigment. Good By this is all at Present. Kiss Baby for me.

Jim McIlhinny is safe Pray for me

Adue your affec Husband
J. H. Pardington

A Kiss

John

1. Battle of Chancellorsville.

undated letter

Dear Sarah for the Want of Paper I take a Peace of Marys letter. Enclosed I send you a five dollar confederate note. It is worth nothing But it will be a novelty. It is a awful dark and Rainy night and our tents leak. Jim McIlheny and me tent together and live together. We are Both in good spirits But would like to see Trenton. I must say good night for the Drums Beat for the Lights to be Put out so good night. God Bless you. Send me a sheet of Paper next [time]. Ask Willie if he received my letter and [ask] him to Write. Your Loveing Husband

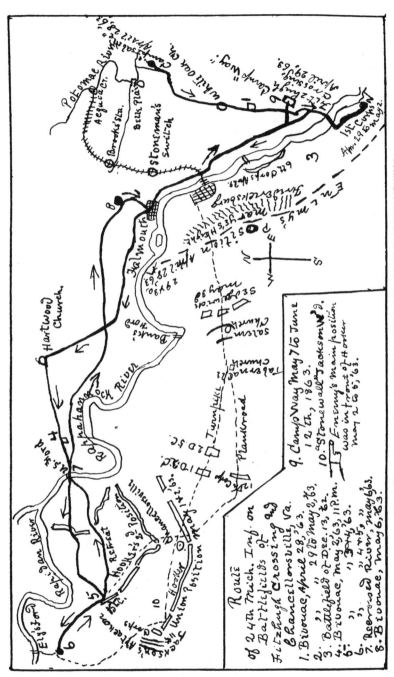

ROUTE OF "IRON BRIGADE" AT FITZHUGH CROSSING AND THE FIELD OF CHANCELLORSVILLE.

Route of Twenty-fourth Michigan Infantry on Battlefields of Fitzhugh Crossing and
Chancellorsville, Virginia.

dear Sarah

Near the Raphannock Falmouth Va
May 8/63

My dear Wife

I received your Welcome letter of the 25th and glad I was to hear from you. Well Sarah we have had a hard time of it these last ten days. We crossed the River but had to fall Back again. It was a terrible Battle in loss of life but we have killed two to our one. But I think they have taken more Prisener[s] than we have. I have come out all right again thank God. We expect every hour to cross again. God only knows the result. We have lost in our Reigment some 20 or 30 Killed or wounded. The loss of life must be awful on Both sides and yet we had to retreat again. Well dear Sarah you said about me buying that house. Well I hardly know what to think. Suppose I should get wounded so it would lay me up then what. I should rather wait till this war is over. Dear Sarah tell me what you think in your next letter. We have lost Asa Brindle. He was from Wyandotte. He clerked in Aubrey['s] store. For eight days we have had no sleep. Only what we could katch at intervals. We have been fighting and working night and day. We are resting a little now and I hope they will for two or three days. The trenton Boys are all right so far. Last Sunday was the hardest fighting we had. I tell you Sarah we lost this fight on account of the 9 months men and two years men. Their times are so near out that they dont [fight]. They Break and Run. But we fell Back in good order. I do hope Sarah that this war will be ended before long But I hardly know what to think of it. Everything seems to work against us. Our Reigment was the first to cross the river. We done it in open Boats and stormed the enemy Rifle Pits. We captured about two hundred Rebs well Sarah I must close. We must get our guns in fighting trims again. So good By my dear Wife and child. May heaven Bless you Both are the Prayers of your affec Husband and Father

J. H. Pardington
A Kiss for Both
Good By

Remember me to all.

Near Raphannock River Va
May 9th 1863

Dear Sister

I have just received your kind and affec letter which was most thankfully received. But Maria I am sorrow to say I can not send my Picture this time. The reason I will tell you. Since I wrote you last we have been fighting and marching all the time. We crossed the Raphannock River on the 27th of April and for ten days we have been fighting. Our Reigment and the 6th Wissconsin were the first to cross. We crossed the River in open Boats and stormed the enemys Rifle Pits at the Point of the Bayonet. We killed and wounded some forty and took some 200 Priseners. We lost in our Reigment some 30 killed and wounded. It was one of the most daring feats of the war. But God in his gracious goodness has spared me from danger and harm. Maria last sunday was the most terrible fighting ever known. The Rebels loss cant fall short of 25000 or 30000. Our loss is large. We had to fall Back across the river again on account of the 11th Army Corp Breaking and Running which caused our Repulse. But the Rebels got the worst of it this time. There was some Places w[h]ere the Rebels lay 6 or 7 deep. We expect to try it again before long in a day or two at least. I tell you Maria them Rebels fight good. I wish they were fighting in a better cause. Now Maria you must not expect a long letter this time. This is merely to let you know that I am safe after one of the most hard fought Battles of the war. The time we were crossing the River I took just as cool aim at the Grey Back as if I was shooting squrrils. They Pick our Reigment to cross first every time. I suppose when we cross again the gallant 24th will have to do it first. Now Maria dear I must say good By. Give my love to all and Beleive me to Be your affec Bro

Corperal J. H. Pardington

Direct the same
I will get my Picture the first oppertunity

John

Camp Near White Oak Church Va
May the 9/63

Friend Willie

I received you[r] letter on the Battle feild last Monday and now we are repulsed and Back across the River. I will hasten to answer it. Well Willie we have a hard time of it this last twelve days. We crossed the River on the 28th day of April. Our Reigment and the 6th Wissconsin were the first to cross in open Boats. We carried the Rebels rifle Pits at the Point of the Baynot [bayonet]. We killed and wounded 40 and took some 200 Prisenors. Our loss was between 20 and 30 killed and wounded. That is our Reigment. The other Reigment lost heavy. Well Willie it was one of the hardest fought Battles of the war and had it not been for the 11th Army Corp running we would have gained the day. I never see such slaughter in my life. The Rebels lay in some Places 7 or 8 deep. Their loss must be 25000 or 30000. Our loss is heavy. We expect to try again before long.

dear Sarah

Well Willie I must soon close for the mail will soon go out. The trenton Boys are all well and safe give my love to all and Beleive me Your Ever Truly

J. H. Pardington

Direct the same

P.S. Our Army is decresing. Ever[y] day troops are leaving By Reigments a day going home their time being out. Tell Sarah I have wrote her since the Battle

John

Respects to Mr Clee and fam.

Camp Near White Oak Church Va
Sunday May 10 1863

Dear Sarah

I received your Welcome letter (may 3rd) last night and was very glad to hear from you and Baby. Dear Sarah when your letter came to me at camp Elias happened to be there. He came over to see me as usual. He is well but cant tell when he will be home. Probily about july or august. There is an enducement held out here for the two years men to enlist over again for one year with $50 dollar Bounty. But he has not decided if he will enlist or not before he come home. Dear Sarah we Both came out safe in the Battle thank God. It was a hard one and terrible slaughter on Both sides. About the house Sarah tell Kittle to hold on and not sell it for I will tell better in about a month from now. For it is likely I shall buy it. So tell him not to speak to any Body else about it. The loss in the six Army Corp the one that Elias was in was about 7000 in all. Our loss alltogether was about 10000 men. The Rebel loss is estimated at 15000. A Pretty Big fight wasant it Sarah. Our Reiginent lost some 30 killed and wounded. I am now with Elias. I staid with him last night. But I shall have to leave him very soon for I must get back to camp before noon. Well Sarah I must close. Have you received the draft. I sent By express $36.00. I hope you have [it]. Well good By my dear Wife and child. May heaven Bless you Both are the Prayers of your affec Husband and Father

Corp J. H. Pardington

Direct the same

P.S. give my love to all at home

John

Elias send[s] his Best Respects and love to all at home and Friends

Camp Near White Oak Church Va
May 13th 1863

Dear Sarah

Haveing nothing to do I thought the best thing I could do was to write a letter to my loved ones at home knowing they are always glad to hear from me. Well dear I have told you of the desperate Battle we had here a few days ago and dear Sarah although we fell Back accross the river we gave them Rebels one of the worst thrashings they ever got from our army since the war commenced and one they will not forget in awhile. We captured 5000 Prisnors and killed and wounded 18000 of their Best troops Besides killing their favorite general [Jackson]. He is dead. We got a official report this morning.[1] So you see dear Sarah we just gave them fits. Our loss is not over 12000 killed wounded and missing. There was one thing that was terrible and that was when the Battle raged the worst. The woods caught *fire* Burning quite a large number of wounded and dead on Both sides. It was awful. On Sunday never was known such terrible fighting in warfare before and Our Gallant Jo Hooker was there. [H]is Headquarters was on Horse Back rideing along the lines of Battle encourageing his men By his Brave and manly face. When he rode Past cheers after cheer went up from the throats of our Brave Boys. Well dear Sarah I am well only a slight cold on my lungs caused By so much exposure and fatange [fatigue]. But I hope to get rid of it in a few days. How is our little Maria. All right I hope. And yourself O how I long to see you dear Sarah. Sarah I came out of Battle unharmed thank God for his mercies toward me. We may stay quite awhile here w[h]ere we are for we have got a nice camp. Dear Sarah I hope you have received that draft safe that I sent By express. Jim McIlhinny sent one the same time as I did. Well Sarah I must close. It is tremendous Hot here now. We cant do anything But lay in the shade but its nice and cool nights. The 24th has Earned a glorious name in this last fight. Do you ever hear from your Brother Will now. What is he doing. Well good By dear Sarah give my best respects to all. Kiss the Baby for me and except the same Kiss and tenderest love from your affec Husband and Father John

Write soon dear

J. H. Pardington

Direct the same

1. After a personal reconnaissance into enemy territory, General "Stonewall" Jackson was fired upon and mortally wounded by one of his own men as he returned to the Rebel lines.

dear Sarah

May 23, 1863

Dear Wife

I received your letter of the 14th last night and you cant tell dear Sarah how much it releived my mind from anxiety for it was the first letter I had got from any of mine before we left the Old camp ground and since the Battle. I [was] very glad to hear that you had got the draft all right. Dear Sarah I have been very sick with the Remittant fever since I wrote you last but I am getting along firstrate again. I tell you dear Sarah I was sick for awhile. I look rather Peekish yet. Our Reigment went out on a nother adventure or scouting but I could not go with them this time on account of my sickness. They started yesterday morning. Some say they are gone for six days. I think that Port Royal is their destination again. Well I hope they will have as good a time as we had before. Come off without the loss of a man. There were five reigments went all together with a Battery of six guns. So I think they will have a little fun before they get Back. Sarah I guess we had Better not buy the House I will tell you why. Down here it is so uncertain I may come out all right and I may lose a arm or leg or be wounded very Bad so it would lay me up and I should hate to get the house half Payed for and then have to lose it. Elias was telling me he would help me all he could But after all dear Sarah we will let it rest till I get home God Willing. Sarah dear do not tell me again about saving much and you allmost get discouraged sometimes to think you cant save more. Now dear Sarah don't talk that way anymore because it Pains me to read it. Sarah I did not leave you there to stint yourself and freting about saveing. I left you there to be comfortable and you shall be if it take every cent I earn and more to. Sarah I earnt a good liveing when I was at home and God grant that I can do it again and thrice happy we will be dear Sarah when we are together again never to leave till death shall Part us. O Sarah I love you and when I am sick it is then I miss you most. No dear Sarah I do not think you extravigant by no means. I want you to look well for you know dear Sarah that I was always tastey was I not dear. O how I do want to see you Both and clasp you Both in my arms never to leave you more. Sarah we will be Happy wont we when I return wont we. I can just fancy to my self the meeting. I know I should cry like a little Baby but it would be for joy though wouldent it my dear. Why Sarah I did not send Miss Long my Picture. How can she say so why don't they answer the letter. I am sorry to hear that Willie has left trenton. But maybe it is all for the best. Now dear Sarah you must give my love to Mr McIlhiny folks and to all I know in trenton. Jim Havens and Wife. Plumb and Wife and Kittles folks and Mr Clees folks. Give my love to your folks at home. Sarah I will let you know in time if I can get a furlough or not this summer. Well I must say good By and may heavens choisest Blessing rest on you Both are the Prayers of your own John. Kiss little Maria for me and except one warm Kiss from your affec Husband

Corperal J. H. Pardington

Direct the same

P.S. it is awful hot here days but cool nights

Camp Near White Oak Church Va
May 24 1863

My dear Sister

I received your most Welcome letter last night and was glad to hear from you again and so quick. Maria you are the most Punctual that I write to from the army. Dear Sister since I wrote you last I have been quite sick with the Remittant fever But thank god I am able again to do duty. Our Reigment is gone off on a Reconisance and scouting for six days. I was not able to go with them. It is the first time that the[y] ever went without me on any accinon [action] But if I had went I should have had to come Back. I never could have stood the marching. Maria it is tremendious Hot down here now I never see weather in Michigan to beat it and this is only *may* wait till it comes July or August then we will get it. Maria I hope to see this war over by fall. I hope to God it will. God know only when. Well Maria there is no signs of an onward movement here yet. We have a nice camp ground here and all we want is a few nice young ladies to cheer us now and then. I guess the girls will think we soldiers rather rough when we get Back not being in their company so long. But then I guess we will behave ourselves Pretty well. How is Ellens sister. Is she married yet. Tell Dick I never will forget the time him and me and George and Ellen and her sister went to a dance and how they give us the mitten right in the street only because me and dick would Put our hands up to the side of our face and wink at one another. That was fun them days I tell you. Ask dick if he remembers when I was going to lick George in the Ball room. I tell you he could not [commit] none of his [sins] over Jack. He has traveled to much. Oh how I would like to see Alf Bob and all of them. It would do me good I tell you. Ask dick if he has forgot how to kis now he knows our Old way (*A,LA,Widow*).

Well Maria I was sorry to hear that your quails had Played the truant and gone. I could not help laughing when I read it. I could just fancy how you Pouted and said (it *is real vexing*) and to Bad. Well maria you must get another kind of *Pet* that wont *fly away*. *No insult though* as George said in his letter one day that his wife could not have any stock so he should have to go raising *canary Birds*. Well that is better than nothing you know. I guess my little stock takes them all down. They say she is a regular finished one. I calculated she would be before hand. Enough of that.

Maria about furlough, I may get one this sumner and I may not. The Captain of our Company has Promised me one But there is two or three ahead of me. Dear Sister never fear if I get one But what I will stop and see you when I Pass through Toledo. Maria do you ever see the Miss Carrs. If you do will you Remember me to them. I have had many a game of checkers with them. Maria if you were here now with me I would give you a glass of Lemonade. There is a young fellow from detroit sitting alongside of me writing and we have some Lemonade By us. Our own makeing but it aint got no slick in it of course not. Maria did I ever tell you that I saw Ed Sackrider[1] since I have been in the army. Such is the case I saw him near Washington last fall. He was in the 17th Michigan. Our Reiginent and theirs lay quite close together. He heard that I was in the 24th so he came over and found me out. I was laying asleep under a shade tree. He awoke me up But I did not know [him] at first. He kept his arm hid from my view. He was so taned and changed. But after I see his arm was off I soon knew him. We had a long talk on home affairs and about you. He thought a good deal of you Maria. He is Post master in the 17th. He told me he expected to get Brigade Postmaster. I hope he got it. I have not seen him since. I shall Probily not see him again for the Reigment went down West under *Burnsides,* I wish him luck. Well Maria to day is Sunday we have a very nice Chaplin with us. He is a near friend of Rayner which makes it more Pleasent for me. We have Preaching every Sunday. That is when we are in Camp and fine weather. Well Maria I must close with kind love to all my friends and Dick Alf Bob Ellen and all and Beleive me to be your Ever Affec Bro John,

Corperal J. H. Pardington

Direct the same

P.S. Maria I am sorry I cannot get my Picture yet for you But I will never fear

John

1. An old beau of his sister, Maria.

Camp Near White Oak Church Va
May 25/63

My Dear Wife

I received your Welcome letter of the 18th and was glad to hear from
you and Baby once more. Well dear Sarah I have recovered from the
affects of my sickness and am Pretty smart again thank God. Sarah that
was a bad affair of Mrs Goodith. I hope they will find out the guilty
Parties and bring them to *justice.* I dont know how I should feel if it
was my case. One thing certain I would know no rest till I would have
their blood and that I would if it took years to get it. But I would revenge
a Wife of mine most *terrible* on a case like that. But God forbid that it
should ever happen to my *dear Wife.* Well dear Sarah there is not much
new here now at Present every thing is quiet on the Rappahanock at Present. But how long it will stay so no one can tell But our Brave leader Jo
Hooker. Sarah when you see your Father again tell him I should like to
hear from him for it is quite awhile since I got a letter from him. I am
sorry to hear about Wills child being sick in Canada but I tell you Sarah
I am afraid he will see a good deal of trouble yet and missfortune. I Bet
his concience trouble him a good [deal] in regard to his desertion. Sarah
I think that this war will soon close now we have splendid news from
Vicksburg. Our General Grant is just giving them fits down there. News
came to *Headquarters* last night that it was taken. I have no doubt it is
true. If it is the Rebellion is on its last legs and in its dying struggle. But
I tell you it dies *hard.* But Our *Glorious flag* shall *triumph* sooner or later.
Three cheers for Our Brave Jo Hooker the Soldiers favorite and stand
By. Well Sarah I long to see you. I love you stronger than I ever loved you
before. God Bless you Both. Yesterday being Sunday we had a very nice
sermon from Leuit. Yemans. You know him. He used to teach school in
trenton and he used to *Preched* [preach] on the west road. Our Reigment
has not come in yet from that Recognacene they went on. We expect
them Back to day or to morrow. They have had a Pretty hard time of it.
By accounts a good many of them were sun struck so you can form some
Idea how hot it is down here alredy. I got another letter from Maria the
other day. She is very Punctual in answering letters and I tell you I am
very glad of it. I wish they were all so my sisters. Sarah about that house
how much can you Pay down on the first Payment. Write and tell me in
your next [letter] with out delay. I suppose that what you let your Father
have you will have no trouble will you. I hope not. Can you get [it] any
time you want it. I would want you to Pay a hundred down the first year
that is right off. Mind you tell me in your next [letter]. I like the house
Sarah and [it] would make us a nice little home wouldent it dear. We
would have *love in a cottage.* I hope you will have no trouble with that

[money] you let your father have but I dont think you will. Oh how I do want to see our little Maria. She must be a beauty I know. Aint she Sarah. Tell Kittle not to sell the house to any body yet till he gets our desision on it. But I want you to tell me in your next how much you can Pay down with that your father owes us. But mind I dont want you to stint yourself and Pay out every cent you got.

Well dear Wife I must close with my kindest love to you and Baby. May Heavens choisest Blessing and Protection rest on your Heads is the Prayer of your affec Husband and Father

J. H. Pardington

Direct the same
Write soon

P.S. Sarah when you see Sarah Banks give James Booths love to her. She will remember him. He called there before the Reigment went away one Sunday with the Miss Hickmott and Mr Weatherspoon.

John

Camp Way
White Oak Church Va
May 29th 1863

Dear Wife

Last night I received your Welcome letter and was much Pleased to hear from dear Wife and *Child*. Your letter found me enjoying good health again Thank God. Sarah we have just had a visit from *Governer Blair* and *Lady* from *Michigan*. The Governer made us quite a nice speech. They left this morning. We are again under Marching Orders to be ready at a moments notice. Of course we do not know where we are Bound to as the sailors say. I guess I shall be able to send you another draft in a day or two. We expect to get Payed to day or to morrow. Sarah there is not much news here now the same old dull life of a soldier when he is in camp. I received the shovel and will ware it for your sake. It is splendid weather here But very warm indeed. I was very sorry to hear of the death of dave Taylors wife. It must be a heavy Blow on him. Poor man I know how heavy a one it would be on me, but God forbid. I received a letter from Willie Sanders the Other day. I dont think he likes the city so well as he do trenton. Sarah I hardly know what to say about a furlough now. You know they need every soldier now a days. I think it will be hard to get one but I will let you know when I can get one. Dear Sarah I get very lonesome sometimes and I know you do but never mind dear I hope the time is not far distant when our lonesomeness will be turned to joyfullness when we meet again to live in each others company and love to each Other. Oh Sarah I often think how we will appreciate each other love in the future. God speed the day is my Prayer and I know dear Sarah it is yours. Oh I want to see you Both so bad but I suppose I shall have to wait Paintently and hope for the best. Sarah I will have to close. Enclosed you will find a draft for 18 dollars. I hope you will get it all right. Good By God Bless you Both. In Haste I remain Your Ever affec Husband

J. H. Pardington

Write soon Direct the same tell me if you get it safe

On Pickett Banks of
Rappahanock River Va
Sunday May 31/63

Dear Sarah

Haveing nothing to do but to keep an eye on the Rebels for we are on Pickett to day on the River Right By where we had such a hard time crossing in this last Battle. So while I keep one eye on the Rebels I will endeavor to keep one on this letter while I am writing it. It is splendid weather down here now. Every thing is so nice and green. It is a splendid looking country down here on the Banks of the River and around frederickburg. We are laying now on what was once *Washington farm.*[1] It is a splendid scenery around here.

June 1st

Well dear Sarah since I comnenced this letter I have just received one from you dated May 24th and was glad as ever to hear from you and Baby. We are still on Pickett and a splendid morning it [is]. I have just had a good Bathe in the water which makes me feel good. Well Sarah it is rather dull here. All we have to do is to whach the *Grey Backs* and they watch us. We are within rifle shot of them. But there is no fireing on Pickett now which makes it more Pleasent. It aint no use for Picketts to fire on one another. It only seems like murder and it dont do any good to either side. Well Sarah we cant tell when we will have another fight. But

dear Sarah

I dont [think] the day is far distant when we will have another one. Well Sarah I should like to see our little darlin sitting on the floor with a dish of water Playing with it. Sarah about that report that came to Wyandotte about my being sick was true but I cant tell who wrote it. In one of my other letters I told you about it. I sent you a draft of 18 dollars the other day. I hope you will get it safe. I suppose everything looks nice around there now. Wheat down here is out. Wheat and corn is high up so you see we are ahead of you here. The trenton boys are all well so far. Jim is well. I should like to be with you Now dear Sarah to go around with you visiting. Wouldent you dear. Well Sarah there is no more news to write at Present. I will have more in the next. So good By my dear Wife and Child. May God Bless you Both are the Prayers of your affec Husband and Father

Corpl J. H. Pardington

Direct the same

P.S. the Paper that you wrote your letter on had some Picture of two girls saying "none But the Brave Deserve the fair" that is true.
Write soon

Jack

1. The farm of the family of George Washington.

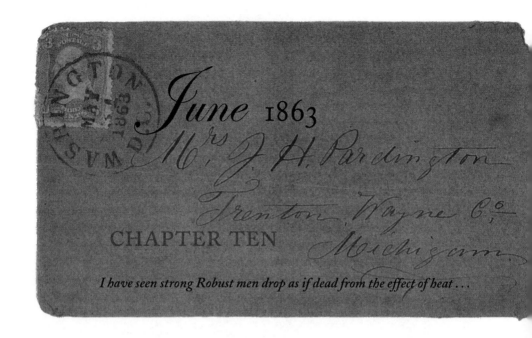

CHAPTER TEN

I have seen strong Robust men drop as if dead from the effect of heat . . .

John's first letter in June sounds quite wistful. Two of the officers' wives were in camp visiting, and John wrote that "just the Sight of a woman in camp makes it more Pleasent whenever I look at them I have to think of you and Home and *sigh* and wish." He also announced that the Iron Brigade had been promoted to First Brigade. It was the "Post of Honor and the most dangerous post in military life." Their designation was now First Corps, First Division, First Brigade of the great Army of the Potomac.

Although John believed that they were getting what they deserved, because they had deserted their country's flag at "this Hour of Peril," he felt sympathy for three or four men who were to be shot: "Poor fellows they have only a day or two more to live." Little did he know that he himself had only a few weeks to live as the army moved inexorably closer to Gettysburg.

Perhaps because we know the end of his life was near, the June letters take on special meaning. As he makes plans for Sarah to buy a house, as he speaks so eloquently of his commitment to his "adopted country" (John was born in England), as he expresses his anger once again toward the Copperheads, and as he bemoans the killing of women and children in Vicksburg, we become aware of a man who has matured immeasurably in the past nine months. Even mundane requests for tobacco and writing paper and his thanks to Sarah for sending a magazine and papers

dear Sarah

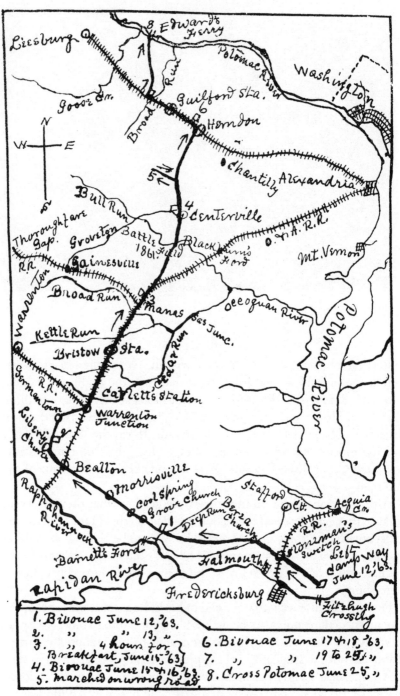

Liesburg · S. Edward's Ferry · Potomac River · Washington · Goose Cr. · Broad Run · Guilford Sta. · 6 · Herndon · 5 · Chantilly · Alexandria · N · W · E · S · Bull Run · 4 · Centerville · O. & A. R.R. · Thoroughfare Gap · Groveton Battle 1861 Field · Black Burn's Ford · Mt. Vernon · R.R. · Gainesville · Warrenton · Broad Run · 3 · Manas · Occoquan River · Kettle Run · Sas. Junc. · Cedar Run · Bristow Sta. · Catlett's Station · German Town · R.R. · Warrenton Junction · Liberty Church · Beallton · Morrisville · Stafford · Acquia Cr. · R.R. · Rappahannock River · Cool Spring · Grove Church · Beza Church · Deep Run · Cr. · Stoneman's Switch · Left Camp Way June 12, '63. · Barnett's Ford · Falmouth · Rapidan River · Fredericksburg · Fitzhugh Crossing · Potomac River

1. Bivouac June 12, '63.
2.   "   "   13, "
3.   "   4 hours for Breakfast, June 15, '63
4. Bivouac June 15 & 16, '63
5. Marched on wrong road.
6. Bivouac June 17 & 18, '63.
7.   "   "   19 to 25, "
8. Cross Potomac June 25, "

The March for Gettysburg.

become poignant. He is also angry and disappointed that the situation between Sarah and her sister, Belinda, with whom Sarah and the baby have been staying, has deteriorated, and John urges her to find other accommodations.

Many of the men of the Twenty-fourth, including John, wrote their last letter home on June 22, 1863. They had been marching north since leaving Camp Way on June 12. By the sixteenth, they were at Bull Run, prompting many members of the Iron Brigade, veterans of that bloody encounter, to reminisce.

The last few days of June saw major changes in the Army of the Potomac. General Hooker, no longer able to endure the criticism of President Lincoln, asked to be relieved of his command. Lincoln had urged Hooker to attack the Rebels where they were vulnerable, saying, "If the head of the beast is in Pennsylvania, and the tail in Virginia, it's body must be mighty slim somewhere." General Meade was the new commander of the Army.

Donald L. Smith, author of *The Twenty-fourth Michigan of the Iron Brigade,* described the last night before the big battle well:

> Four miles down Marsh Creek, south of Gettysburg, the Twenty-fourth Michigan's bivouac was becoming quiet. Fires were dying, men were sleeping, officers were checking last minute reports which the cavalry had given them that afternoon. Finally, they too sought repose, and the gallant men from Detroit and Wayne County, fell into a fitful slumber, the great black hats, which they had never worn in combat, carefully placed beside them. Thus the actors approached the stage. Gettysburg would be the scene. The drama would be done in overtones of gray, shot through with red. The Iron Brigade, Cutler's brigade, and Battery B, were heading the cast. The overture was playing, and soon, all too soon, the curtain would rise on the first act. Tomorrow would be July 1, 1863.

Camp Way Near White Oak Church Va
June 3 1863

Dear Wife and Daughter

Seeing I have nothing to do I dont think I can improve my time any Better than writing to you. Dear Sarah I love to write to you and to receive letters from you. We are off Pickett now and in our *Camp* again. Sarah do you remember one year ago the 11th of this month. I do. Our little Darling will be one year old. God Bless her. Oh how I would love to see her But not worse than I want to see you dear. Well Sarah we are not doing much of anything here. We cant tell when we will march again But we are likely to at any moment we cant tell. Sarah time Passes very quick soldiering. It seems to me it is the shortest nine months I ever see. But I think if I was in your Plase it would seem long. But it is different here with us. We have so many changes it makes the time feel short. I think when I get home again it will be hard for me to go to work again for soldiering is very lazy work. We have two Ladies in camp now. Cap Rexford wife of our Company and Leiutenant Col Flanigans Wife. I tell you Sarah just the Sight of a woman in camp makes it more Pleasent. When ever I look at them I have to think of you and Home and *sigh* and wish But that is all the good it does. But never mind Sarah this war aint agoing to last for ever is it. I hope the time is not far distant when I shall once more feel your warm and *loveing* kiss on my *lips* and your arms around me. Wont we be Happy and appreciate each other love Dear Sarah when [we] meet again. God Hasten the time is the Prayer of your John. Well dear Sarah I think we will Buy that house. It will be a nice little home for us wont it. It will be near a good school for our little one to go to school when she gets Big enough. Well dear Sarah there is not much news to write. When there is I will be sure and tell you. There [are] 3 or 4 men to be shot in our Corp for desertion on the 5th of this month. Poor fellows they have only a day or two more to live. But it is what they deserve. Any man that will desert his countrys flag at this Hour of Peril Deserves to be shot. It will be an example for others. Well dear Sarah good By May God Bless you Both are the Prayers of your affec Husband and Father

J. H. Pardington
Co. B 24 Mich Vol
1st Brigade 1st Division
1st Army Corp
Washington D.C.

P.S. Our Brigade has got Promoted to the first Brigade. It is the Post of Honor. The Post of Honor means the most dangerous Post in Military life.

Camp Near White Oak Church Va
Fryday June 5/63

My dear Wife

Last night I received your ever Welcome letter and was glad as ever
to hear from you and baby and glad to hear that you Both keep well
which dear Sarah is a great Blessing to you. Yesterday morning we were
ordered to strike tents and be ready to march at a moments notice. Well
we done so and went to work and had real fun throwing all our stuff away
what we could not carry on a march such as beans, and Potatoes, molasses, and extra Pork, and one thing and another. And just as we had got
through with our fun and throughed every thing away then the Order
was Countermanded and so we are in our camp. Wasnted it to Bad after
throughing all our extra stuff away and then not going after all because
what we did through away comes usefull when we are in camp. But we
cant carry it on a march. Sarah there is a good deal of talk that we are
going to fall Back on Washington again. I suppose till our army gets
bigger. I do not know how true it will be. But I think the Rebels are trying to get between us and Washington. If it is the case we shall Probily
have a nother fight at *Bulls Run*. That is a lucky Battle feild for the
Rebels. If we should have one there I hope it will Prove lucky for us this
time. I should not be at all surprised Dear Sarah of haveing another
fight there before long too. God Prosper Our arms if we do for we are on
the *Right Side* and (Right is might) we all know. Well dear Sarah we have
just come off Drill. I am enjoying good health again thank God. Yes dear
Sarah I do miss your kind care when I am sick but I must bare up with
soldiers fortitude. When I get home and am sick you will make up for
loss time wont you. Sarah I wish you would send me Maria [the baby]
likeness when she is a year old. For I dont think it is hardly Possible for
me to come home this summer for they need every man they got and I
dont think its my duty to leave now when we are needed the most. Although dear Sarah I want to see you very much. My adopted country
needs me more. Not as I love you less than the good old flag But I love
that next to you and will stick by it as long as she waves for it is the only
flag of the free and will yet triumph over all other *rags* that are afloat
against us now and ever. Well Sarah I must close. Sarah you never told
me how you get your drafts cashed. Do you have to go to Detroit to get
it. Tell me in your next. Well good By God Bless you Both are the Prayers
of your John

J.H. Pardington
Direct as before

dear Sarah

Write soon for I love to hear from you. Trenton Boys are all well. Kiss for you Both

John

Camp Near White Oak Church Va
Sunday June 7 1863

Dear Father

It is a long while since I wrote to you and longer since I have received a letter from you But I hope you will answer this for I would like to hear from you. Well dear Father we are under marching order to move at a minutes notice. Some Portion of the army has moved and gone across the River. There was quite heavy cannonading on the right yesterday. We had our tents struck guns stacked and every thing ready for [a] move. There is another fight in Progress and Before tomorrow morning we may be into it hot and heavy. But I tell you what it is Father. We soldiers dont care of the fire in front of us But we dont know what to make of the fire that will soon happen in our Rear. I mean these Copperhead meatings that are crying for *Peace* at all sacrifice, they seem Bound for Peace if it sacrifices the *Union*. It seem Poor Encouragement for us. While we are fighting for the union they are fighting to have it *Divided*. Sometimes I allmost feel afraid for our *cause*. I see they have had a tremendious Peace meating in *New York* Denouncing the Administration and the President and Cabinet. What give the South Peace as long as they are in arms against us. (never) I say War is the only thing that will bring Peace and safety to the country. Fight them as long as they are in [the] army. How would we look in the eyes of a foregn Power if we should give in now when we are crowding them at all Points. Now is just the time the Coperheads are beginning to rise now they see we are getting the Better of them. But I hope there is enough Loyal men in the north to Put down such Proceding and they ought to be Put down at all hasard. Mark my words if it aint Put down quick there will be trouble ahead and that before long. But God forbid that blood will be spilt north. There is enough spilt here but we are spilling it here in a good cause. I hope they will have no trouble about the draft. But I am afraid it will be resisted in a good many places. But men we must have are [or] our cause is hopeless. The conscript acts is what have made the south so strong. It will be the saveing of our *Glourious flag* and country. Well Father I must close. I shall Probily have some stirring news to tell you in my next if my life is spared. So good By God Bless you all are the Prayers of your affec son

Corperal J. H. Pardington

Direct the same

Kiss my little one for me when you see it and Sarah

John

Elias I suppose is with you now. No more for it is almost church time and I must go and get my dinner and go.

John

Write soon

Camp Near White Oak Church Va
June 9 1863

My dearest Wife

Last night I received your ever Welcome letter and was so muched Pleased to hear from *you* and *Baby*. Well dear Sarah we have not moved yet. We are all ready too. A Portion of our Troops are across the river again. I beleive I could fight better in any other spot But across that river. It is a Perfect slaughter Pen to our foarces. We expect every hour to be called into action. Pray for me dear Sarah to God to spare my life and Permit me to return to my loved ones at home and there to spend the rest of my life in happyness and contentment with *you* and my dear *Daughter*. Wont we be happy when we are together again. Dear Sarah I know you say yes dear John we will be so happy.

Sarah about that house you have my free consent to buy it Tell your Father to use his own judgement and to buy it fore me. It will be a nice little home for us. Tell him if Kittle will take the colts and let it go on the house to let him have them. Tell your Father I would like to have him do the business for me. Tell him to manage it for me as if I was there and he will greatly oblige his Boy John. Tell him I will try and be a good Boy. I have not been in the gaurd house since I have been in the army and dont entend to. I suppose Mr Plumb will stay in the house if you Buy it. I would like to have him stay first rate. Now Sarah let me give you a small bit of advice. If Plumb should move out of the house Be very carefull who [you] let the half of the house too. Dont let it to any Body with a large family and none But respectible folks. But tell Mrs Plumb I should like to have them stay all the time because they are good company for you and the Baby. Sarah do you attend church. I hope you do go as often as you can dear and if God spares my life to come Back to you I shall make it my duty to attend church more than I use to for it is our duty Sarah to God and man. Sarah you let your father read this letter so he can see what I say about the house. I got a letter from him the other night. But I sent one to him this morning before I got it so I will not write him one yet But I guess I will write him a note and send it in this letter.

dear Sarah

Sarah will you go into Mr Parks and Buy a little fine cut Tobaco and ask Mr Park to Press it in a newspaper for you and seal it and Direct it for me. I dont want you to Put to much in so it will make it Bulky so it will keep me in Tobaco. For Tobaco is a thing we need in the army. It is company for us Perticular when we are on Pickett Post. So now Sarah I will not write no more now. I will Probily have more news in my next. So good By God Bless you Both are the Prayers of your affec Husband and Father

J.H. Pardington

Direct the same
A kiss for Both
Write soon
Write soon
Write soon
Write soon
Write soon
Write soon

Headquarters 24th Michigan Volenteers
June 9, 1863

My dearest Wife

I have just received your ever Welcome letter of the 4th which told me you had received the *draft* all right in which I am glad to hear. Sarah I am much obliged to you for your Promtness in answering my letters. I sent you one this morning. But seeing I got one to night I will answer it with Pleasure for I am allways anxious and uneasy till I get your letter answered and when I get it off I feel more at rest. Sarah I am like you. I think Jim Kittridge was in rather of a hurry. But then I guess he was hard *upp* you know. Well Sarah I am writing By candle light in my tent. The reason I write to night is we don't know what minute we may be called to arms. There was heavy fireing just before sundown. But it did not last long. We still have good news from *Vicksburg.* I am confident [that] our forces will capture it before long. I see in the Papers that we have killed quite a number of woman and children in the city by our shell and shot. It seem hard dont it Sarah. But I suppose they thought because they had the woman and children and Vickburg our foarces would not shell the city. But they have got the wrong man to deal with Genl Grant. I am sorry for the woman and children but such is *war.* You say in your letter that you have not been down to Joes nor I dont want you to either. I will let them see after useing you so. You know dear Sarah when they miss use you you no they miss use me. Aint that so. It may seem hard Dear Sarah But it will show them they have not done you *Justice.* Well Sarah there is

Head quarters 24th Michigan Volenteers
June 9th 1863

My dearest Wife

I have just received your ever Welcome
letter of the 4th which told me you had
received the draft - all right - in which
I am glad to hear. Sarah I am much
obliged to you for your Promtness in
answering my letters. I sent you one this
morning But seeing I got one to night
I will answer it with Pleasure. for I am
allways anxious and uneasy till I get your
letter answered and when I get it off
I feel more at rest. Sarah I am like you I think
Jim Kittridge was in rather of a hurry But
then I guess he was hard upp you know,
well Sarah I am writing By candle light
in my Tent - the reason I write to night is
we dont know what minute we may be
called to arms there was heavy fireing
just before sundown. But it did not
last long. we still have good news

dear Sarah

from Vicksburg I am confident that our force
will capture it before long I see in the Papers
that we have killed quite a number of
woman and children in the city by our
shell and shot it seem hard dont
it Sarah. But I suppose they thought because
they had the woman and children in Vicks
burg our forces would not shell the city
But they have got the wrong man to deal
with Genl Grant. I am sorry for the
woman and children but such is war
you say in your letter that you have not
been down to Joes nor I dont want you
too either I will let them see after use
in you so. you know dear Sarah when
they misuse you. you no they miss
use me aint that so, it may seem hard
Dear Sarah. But it will show them they have not
done you justice, well Sarah there is nothing
news here so I will come to a close Wishing
a good night and Pleasent dreams so good
night my dear may heavens choisest Bles
in rest on you my dear Wife and children
are the Prayers of your affec Husband
and father

Jno H. Pardington

not much news here so I will come to a close Whishing a good night and Pleasent dreams. So good night my dear may heavens choisest Blessing rest on you my dear *Wife* and *child* are the Prayers of your affec Husband and Father

J. H. Pardington

Bull Run Near Centerville
June 16/63

My dear Wife

You will no doubt stare when you see w[h]ere we are. But we are on the Bloody feild of Bull Run. But we are [abreast] of the Rebels and have got a good Position so let them come. We are ready for them Sarah. I am not going to write much of a letter now Because we are all excitement and dont know when we will move. Maybe before night. We have suffered a good deal of Hardshipe since I Wrote you last. We have had some terrible marching night and day. I have seen strong Robust men drop as if dead from the effect of heat and fatauge. But thank God I stood it firstrate only a little foot sore. I have not straggled a foot on the last march because it is awful Bad to be left behind and to ketch up after. It is tremendious Hot and dusty. We have had no rain to speak of this last six or seven weeks. We get very hard up for water in this Part of the country. We suffered some on this last march Drinking water that would turn the stomich any other time. But a soldier has to drink anything. Sarah I have drank water out of a ditch when there [h]as been a Dead horse laying a few rods above in the same Water and glad to get it. Sometimes we make coffee of water when it looks has [as] if it was half milk so mudy. It is [a] wonder more soldiers dont die than do just through drinking such water. Well Sarah I must close. This is only to tell you w[h]ere we are and what we are doing. One thing we have got some Hardships ahead of us. Kiss little Maria for me and except one for yourself and Beleive me to be your ever faithful Husband and Father

John H. Pardington

Direct the same
Remember me to all
Write soon

Camp Near Guilford Station va
June 22/63

My dear Wife

I received three letters from you at once in which I will answer in this one. Dear Sarah it is with Pleasure I read them. I received 7 letters at once. One from your Father and the rest from different ones. Sarah it is hard for us to get letters or to send them off. You see we are after the enemys now. There was hard fighting about 8 miles ahead of us about 7 miles yesterday it being Sunday which is a favorite day for fighting in the army. I suppose they think Better the day Better the deed. We expect every day to be at it. There has got to be hard fighting done this summer. But I do hope that this summer will see it ended. God knows there has been enough Blood spilt in this curssed War. Well dear Sarah I had a letter from Elias. He is in Alexandria working at his trade. I may have a chance to see him this summer and [h]is girl. I have seen her likeness. She is quite a good looking girl and will make him a good Wife. Now Sarah if you dont get a letter very often from me this summer you must not feel to down hearted about it because on a campaign like we are on now we cannot get a chance to send a letter off or hardly receive one. But dear Sarah you are in my thoughts all the time and your Picture I cover with kisses But it wont kiss me Back again. But never mind dear you will kiss me when I get home *God Willing* wont you. You say Belinda is as good as Pie now. I dont like her any the better for that nor I do not want you to visit them at all. Nor any of them down that way. Sarah you may think me hard. But Sarah they have used you to Bad for me to relent or forgive them till I know the cause or they will write to me about it. I think it was Joes duty to write me and tell me all about it when it first commenced. But enough of that. Now dear Sarah dont forget to send me some Tobaco for it is scarce here. So Bill is living in Trenton. Does he work the farm yet. Sarah Did Willie ever Pay you that five dollars yet for that Pistol I sent him. Sarah I received three Papers this time and was very glad to. I received from you a magazine too. Well Sarah I must now close with kind [regards] to all Kiss our little darling for me and send me her likeness. Sarah dear I was sorry to hear you were not well But do hope that you will be well when this reaches you. I am enjoying good health thank God. So now good By my dear may God Bless you Both are the Prayers of your affec Husband and Father

J. H. Pardington

Write soon
Love to all excuse this scrawl
Send me a small sheet of Paper every time you write

John

[This was John's last letter.]

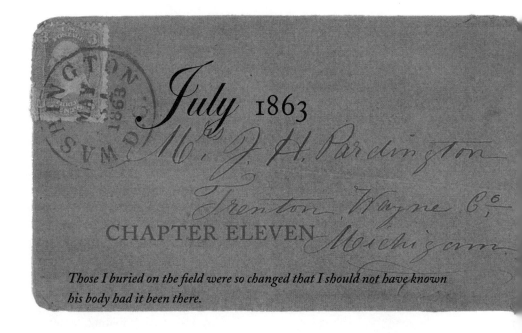

CHAPTER ELEVEN

Those I buried on the field were so changed that I should not have known his body had it been there.

We approach July 1 with feelings of trepidation. Sometime during the next twelve hours or so Cpl. John Pardington gave his "last full measure of devotion." There is a sense of wanting to reach back through the ages and warn him, or somehow protect him from his fate.

Early that Wednesday morning they ate their usual breakfast of hardtack, pork, and coffee, and Chaplain Way began the day with prayers. Having no idea that their first encounter would be so soon, their mood was quite lighthearted until word arrived for General Meredith, leader of the Iron Brigade, that, in front of them, the Union cavalry had met the enemy and were in desperate need of support from the First Corp.

The pace quickened down the Emmitsburg road while the men loaded their guns and fixed bayonets. A mile short of town the brigade left the road to continue through the woods and forests. Here, in a hail of bullets, they met Archer's Tennessee Brigade. The *New York Tribune* described it:

> Reynolds [General Reynolds, leader of the First Corp] has ridden into the angle of wood, a bow-shot from the Seminary, and cheers the Iron Brigade as they wheel on the flank of the oak trees for a charge. Like a great flail of steel they swing into the shadows with a huzza that is terrible; low, crouching by his horse's head, the General peeps into the depths of the grove. "Boom" from the oaken recesses breaks a hail-

The Old Flag.

storm of lead, and Reynolds, with the word of command upon his tongue, falls forward. The architect of the battle has fallen dead across its portal!

Across the brook and up the hill, out from the wooded ravine, two jagged arcs leap into sight. Huzza! From the skirts of the oak the great double doors of the Iron Brigade shut together, with a slam as if of colliding mountains, folding between them 1500 rebel prisoners of war.

During this charge the Twenty-fourth suffered many losses. There were many lines of battle formed that day; fighting and protecting the bullet-riddled flag became a cause in itself. Four or five men were killed as each in turn picked up the colors to rally the men. The dead included Sergeant Abel Peck, the color-bearer, and among the wounded was Lt. Col. Mark Flanigan, who lost his leg. Colonel Morrow himself rescued the colors between color guards. At the sixth line of battle, Colonel Morrow, holding the flag high, received a serious head wound. It was probably about this time that Pardington fell. A deeply moving excerpt from the diary of Pvt. Edward A. Raymor, also of Company B, dated July 3, 1863, says,

> Gettysburg terrible. Advanced double quick on the 1st and did not have time to load guns. Fighting in the woods lasted over 1 hour. Standing 20 paces from the rebs we fired continuous volleys. Lost Price and Cline. Lost my way in confusion when I heard Carroll cry out. Heard he is dead now. I killed 14 rebs. Shot the one who killed John Pardington. Lieutenant Buell rebuked me for drinking after. Said I would not be promoted. I do not care.

Captain Edwards took command and, carrying the flag, bravely led

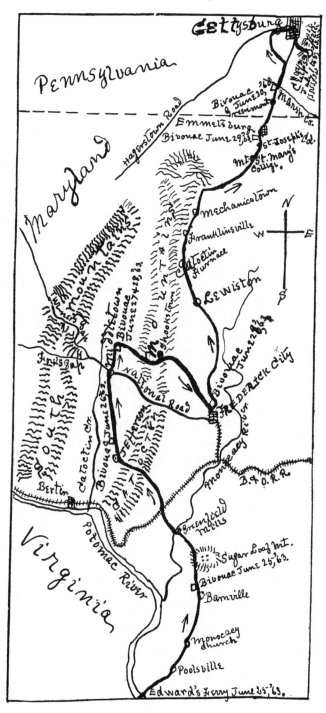

The March to Gettysburg.

the remnants of the Twenty-fourth to a new position overlooking the town of Gettysburg. That morning 496 men had gone into action. That evening only ninety-nine men and three officers were able to respond to a muster.

Although they were forced to fall back, the day was considered a victory because precious positions were preserved that enabled the Union army to triumph on July 3. The Twenty-fourth Michigan received high praise from General Wadsworth when he said, "Col. Morrow, the only fault I find with you is that you fought too long, but God only knows what would have become of the Army of the Potomac if you had not held the ground as long as you did."

Of course, word of the great battle had reached Detroit, and family members were desperately worried about their loved ones. Dread increased for Sarah when no letters arrived from her husband. She asked close friend Willie Sanders to inquire about John. He wrote to Chaplain Way and received a letter from him dated August 19, 1863, in which the chaplain explained why he was unsure of John's whereabouts. Because the dead and wounded lay on the battlefield for many days, identification was impossible for some. We have a document indicating that John was fatally shot in the right chest. We can only assume that he is buried in an unmarked grave somewhere in Gettysburg. On July 9, the *Detroit Advertiser and Tribune* printed a letter from a minister, George Duffield, who had gone to the battlefield to help with the dead and wounded. In part, it said, "The scene of their severest fighting was in a beautiful grove, covered now with graves as thickly as in a cemetery, and nearly all the trees are bullet scarred. Many of the graves of our fallen are marked, but many are unrecognizable."

John's best friend, James McIlhiny, survived. Perhaps he is the one who sent home John's locket with pictures of John and Sarah. Or perhaps the locket I have was Sarah's. We don't know, but they are the only pictures we have of them, and the letters frequently mention the "likenesses" they have of each other.

The losses of the Twenty-fourth Michigan Infantry were the greatest of the Union forces at Gettysburg. When they left Detroit on August 29, 1862, they were 1,030 strong. At a muster one year later 185 men appeared. To honor their bravery, the remnants were asked to serve as part of the Honor Guard at President Abraham Lincoln's funeral in April 1865.

Gettysburg Aug 19/63

Mr. W. Sanders[1]

Dear Sir you have been surprised at my silence in regard to your letter of the 17th and will be surprised at an answer this late date. I received a package of letters from the regt last eve (27) and among them the one from you. I have not been with the regt since the battle but have been here and hence did not get your letter, as I anticipated leaving and joining my regt and hence did not have my mail forwarded to me.

In my report of the Killed and Wounded I did not mention the name of your friend Pardington because I could not ascertain any thing definite concerning him and now I am just as much in doubt and cannot give you any information positive. I hope you have heard from him in this. Those I buried on the field were so changed that I should not have known his body had it been there. He may be a prisoner. I hope so for the sake of his family and may God bless them.

I Am Yours Truly
William C. Way

1. "Willie" Sanders was the dear friend Sarah turned to when John's letters stopped after the Battle of Gettysburg. Sanders wrote to Chaplain Way to inquire about John.

Freind Sarah

Wm Way does not seem to know much about poor John, but I guess the news is to true. I left the Island Wednesday Morning. Give my Respects to all.

From Your Freind
Wm Sanders

dear Sarah

There Has Been a Battle

There has been a battle, as the words along the lines come thrilling,
The mighty East and West and North, with the giant echo filling;
And all along the busy street, amid the rush and rattle,
The hurrying men pause as they meet, to say, "There has been a battle."

Sitting in idle quiet here, in my low chamber lonely,
Their eager voices meet my ear, but not their voices only,
The loitering breezes o're and o're are telling me the story,
Of faces that shall come no more, and battlefields all gory.

Of brave men in the carnage killed, still on the red ground lying,
And hospitals whose wards are filled with true hearts slowly dying;
And forms the noblest of the North, who fought and faltered never,
That must from those dear wards go forth as crippled forms forever.

And lightly borne across the moor, by the low south wind sweeping,
There comes to me from many a door, the voice of many weeping;
Weeping above their battle dead, in hopeless, helpless sorrow;
Refusing to be comforted through faith in any morrow.

By M. W. Edgar

*The Iron Brigade Fighting against Three Lines of Battle at McPherson's Woods
in the Battle of Gettysburg, July 1, 1863.*

Defending the Colors at Gettysburg, July 1, 1863.

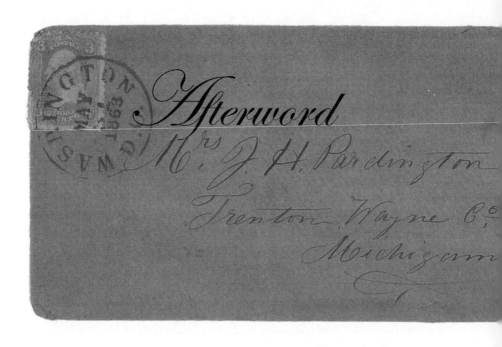

Afterword

After reading the last of John's letters and Chaplain Way's letter, one is left with a feeling of great loss, not only for John but for all the Union and Confederate men who lost their lives in the War between the States. One wonders, also, what happened to Sarah and her daughter, Maria. Sarah remarried twice. In October 1864 she wed Robert McDonald (the Bob McDonald whom John mentioned in his first letter). They had more children. After Robert's death in 1902, she married his brother, George McDonald. This was more a marriage of convenience, as George had lived with his brother and sister-in-law for many years, and it was considered unseemly for a single man and a single lady to live together. She lived a long life and was loved and deeply respected by her family and friends.

Maria grew up and married Frederick Arthur Peel. Their union produced five sons. Between 1888 and 1905, Maria suffered the profound loss of her husband and three of her sons, all in separate accidental deaths. Two of her sons, Frank and Weymouth, died in infancy, while her eldest son, Arthur, drowned on the eve of his graduation from high school. Her husband, a chief engineer for the Michigan Central Railroad, died of injuries sustained on the job. Left with two sons, Robert, a toddler, and Fred, a high school senior, she left Detroit and bought a large house in Ann Arbor, Michigan, which she turned into a boardinghouse for male students from the University of Michigan. This enabled her to manage financially and send her older son to the university. Maria had a long-standing deep respect for higher education. (Many years later her son Robert would become a university professor.) The three—Maria, Fred, and Robert—were a close-knit family; after his father's death, Fred became a surrogate father to his little brother.

My father, Robert Lincoln Peel, was given his middle name in honor of one of his mother's heroes, Abraham Lincoln. When Robert reached school age, Maria found a job as a truant officer for the county. Later on, she became a Friend of the Court, working with delinquents and families at risk. She was deputized and issued a gun so she could accompany the troubled young teens to the reform school. She rode around the county in a horse and buggy, which she later replaced with a little car.

Along the way, besides growing professionally, Maria made her mark in other areas. She helped organize one of the first YWCAs and also served on its National Board. She was a strong advocate of family planning and was a member of the Business and Professional Women's group. One of her favorite charities was an Indian school located in northern Michigan. The plight of the American Indian children concerned her deeply, and she became personally involved with the mission. She also became very active in the Women's Suffrage Movement and the Women's Christian Temperance Union.

Maria was highly respected, a great source of strength in the family, and a marvelous role model, especially for her five grandchildren, all girls. Although she had a rather stern outer appearance and displays of affection were rare, we knew she loved and approved of us. She made us proud to be women and, because of her pioneering spirit, we knew that with hard work we, also, could achieve our goals. John Pardington would have been justly proud of his "Baby Maria."

Maria Pardington Peel, 1898, age 36. Photo taken by oldest son Frederick, who was 15 at this time.

Sarah Ann Knapp Pardington McDonald, taken in her senior years (date unknown).

Appendix

Original Members of the Twenty-fourth Michigan Infantry

RANK AND NAME	NATIVITY AND AGE	OCCUPATION AND RESIDENCE	APPOINTED
FIELD AND STAFF			1862
Col. Henry A. Morrow	Virginia, 33	Lawyer, Detroit	Aug. 15
Lt. Col. Mark Flanigan	Ireland, 37	Butcher, Detroit	Aug. 15
Major Henry W. Nall	England, 31	Clerk, Detroit	Sept. 4
Adjt. James J. Barns	New York, 30	Journalist, Detroit	Aug. 15
QUARTERMASTER			
Digby V. Bell, Jr	Pennsylvania, 32	U.S. Cust'm, Detroit	July 26
SURGEON			
Dr. John H. Beech	New York, 35	Physician, Coldwater	Aug. 24
ASSISTANT SURGEON			
Dr. Charles C. Smith	N. Hampshire, 34	Physician, Redford	Aug. 15
SECOND ASSISTANT SURGEON			
Dr. Alexander Collar	New York, 40	Physician, Wayne	Aug. 18
CHAPLAIN			
Rev. William C. Way	New York, 38	Minister, Plymouth	Aug. 19
NONCOMMISSIONED STAFF			
SERGEANT MAJOR			
Edwin E. Norton	Michigan, 25	Clerk, Detroit	Aug. 16
QUARTERMASTER SERGEANT			
Alonzo Eaton	New York, 26	Clerk, Detroit	Aug. 17

COMMISSARY SERGEANT

Gilbert A Dickey	Michigan, 19	Farmer, Marshall	Aug. 17

HOSPITAL STEWARD

Elmer D. Wallace	England, 18	Clerk, Detroit	July 25

CHIEF MUSICIAN

James F. Raymond	New York, 36	Artist, Detroit	Aug. 13

DRUM MAJOR

Daniel B. Nichols	Unknown, 49	Unknown, Detroit	Aug. 17

FIFE MAJOR

Charles Phillips	Unknown, 50	Unknown, Detroit	July 26

Company A

RANK AND NAME	NATIVITY AND AGE	OCCUPATION AND RESIDENCE	ENLISTED
OFFICERS			1862
Capt. Edwin B. Wight	Detroit, 24	Lumberman, Detroit	July 26
1st Lt. Richard S. Dillon	New York, 32	Molder, Detroit	July 26
2d Lt. H. Rees Whiting	Detroit, 25	Journalist, Detroit	July 26
SERGEANTS			
1. Barrett B. Holstead	New Jersey, 28	Printer, Detroit	July 28
2. William J. Nagle	Detroit, 23	Machinist, Detroit	July 29
3. Wendell Benster	New York, 50	Wheelwright, Ash	July 26
4. Gilman Gilson	Maine, 37	Ship Carp'r, Detroit	Aug. 5
5. Edward B. Wilkie	Detroit, 20	Machinist, Detroit	Aug. 12
CORPORALS			
1. Hyacinth Clarke	Ireland, 25	Laborer, Detroit	July 30
2. Augustus F. Ziegler	Detroit, 18	Clerk, Detroit	Aug. 4
3. Menzo M. Benster	Michigan, 22	Miller, Ash	Aug. 9
4. William C. Bates	Detroit, 18	Clerk, Detroit	Aug. 12
5. George A. McDonald	Walpole, Isl. 20	Sailor, Detroit	July 28
6. Mark T. Chase	Canada, 26	Farmer, Brownstown	Aug. 4
7. Fred'k A. Hanstien	Detroit, 18	Shoemaker, Grosse Pte.	July 26
8. Alfred Rentz	Switzerland, 22	Tinsmith, Detroit	Aug. 8
BUGLER			
George M. Kemp	Monroe Co., 20	Farmer, Exeter	Aug. 8
DRUMMER			
George F. Hamilton	New York, 18	Sailor, Detroit	July 26

WAGONER

| Nelson Oakland | Canada, 37 | Calker, Detroit | Aug. 7 |

PRIVATES

Harrison Baker	New York, 30	Carpenter, Flat Rock	Aug. 9
Christopher Beahm	Germany, 18	Farmer, Springwells	July 24
Solomon S. Benster	Michigan, 18	Machinist, Ash	Aug. 2
Wm. H. Blanchard	New York, 20	Farmer, Flat Rock	Aug. 6
Herman Blankertz	Germany, 18	Clerk, Detroit	July 25
Frank Brennon	New York, 22	Farmer, Detroit	July 31
Francis Brobacker	France, 45	Laborer, Detroit	Aug. 1
Roderick Broughton	Ohio, 26	Farmer, Flat Rock	Aug. 4
Harvey J. Brown	New York, 28	Painter, Holly	Aug. 12
Philip Bussing	New York, 36	Farmer, Ash	Aug. 12
Dennis Carroll	Ireland, 23	Farmer, Wayne Co.	Aug. 12
Joseph Carroll	Chicago, 21	Sailmaker, Detroit	Aug. 11
Oscar N. Castle	Oakland, 27	Farmer, Wayne Co.	Aug. 12
John Chandler	Tennessee, 18	Gilder, Detroit	Aug. 12
Garrett Chase	Brownstown, 27	Farmer, Brownstown	Aug. 7
Jonathan D. Chase	Brownstown, 20	Farmer, Brownstown	Aug. 4
Charles Conlisk	Monroe Co., 23	Farmer, Ash	Aug. 6
Max Couture	Detroit, 21	Mason, Detroit	Aug. 7
John S. Coy, Jr.	Ohio, 20	Mason, Lexington	Aug. 4
Dexter B. Crosby	Livonia, 25	Farmer, Groveland	Aug. 12
Lewis Cummons	New York, 18	Farmer, Wayne Co.	July 28
Christopher Daniels	Ireland, 24	Laborer, Detroit	Aug. 12
Alexis DeClaire	Belgium, 19	Tailor, Detroit	Aug. 7
George Dingwall	New York, 18	Farmer, Wayne Co.	Aug. 11
John Dingwall	New York, 20	Farmer, Wayne Co.	Aug. 11
Charles Dubois	Detroit, 23	Mason, Detroit	Aug. 8
William Dusick	Bohemia, 20	Cabinetmaker, Detroit	July 29
George Eldridge	New York, 18	Fanner, Redford	July 29
Daniel F. Ellsworth	Lenawee Co., 18	Farmer, Cambridge	Aug. 5
Charles Fellratt	Wayne Co., 18	Tinsmith, Detroit	Aug. 9
Jacob Fischer	Germany, 44	Saddler, Detroit	Aug. 8
Charles W. Fuller	New York, 25	Clerk, Detroit	Aug. 8
Peter N. Girardin	Detroit, 19	Ship carp'r, Detroit	July 24
Patrick Gorman	Ireland, 18	Farmer, Ash	Aug. 12
Ignace Haltar	Wurtemburg, 21	Tinsmith, Detroit	July 26
Henry Hanstien	Wisconsin, 20	Blacksmith, Grosse Pte.	Aug. 8
John Happe	Prussia, 20	Laborer, Detroit	Aug. 4

James P. Horen	Monroe Co., 23	Farmer, Exeter	Aug. 12
Augustus Jenks	New York, 40	Farmer, Ash	Aug. 12
Lewis E. Johnson	Canada, 18	Laborer, Detroit	July 30
Stephen Kavanaugh	Grosse Isle, 22	Farmer, Exeter	Aug. 12
William Kendall	Detroit, 18	Molder, Detroit	Aug. 12
Charles Lature	Detroit, 18	Woodturner, Detroit	Aug. 7
Anthony Long	Prussia, 23	Farmer, Wayne Co.	Aug. 12
Thomas Mercer	New York, 19	Steward, Detroit	Aug. 9
George A. Moores	Monroe Co., 22	Staveworker, Ash	Aug. 9
Michael Moren	Germany, 34	Laborer, Detroit	Aug. 6
James Murphy	Monroe Co., 20	Farmer, Exeter	Aug. 6
Walter S. Niles	New York, 20	Laborer, Lexington	Aug. 4
Barnard Parish	Monroe Co., 24	Farmer, Ash	Aug. 6
Albert Peyscha	Bohemia, 20	Locksmith, Detroit	July 29
Robert Phillips	Michigan, 21	Farmer, Tuscola	Aug. 7
Alexander G. Picard	Detroit, 23	Painter, Detroit	Aug. 11
Frank Picard	Canada, 24	Carpenter, Detroit	Aug. 6
Stephen Prairie	Monroe Co., 22	Farmer, Ash	Aug. 6
Charles Quandt	Germany, 28	Farmer, Hamtramck	Aug. 6
William Rouseau	New York, 21	Sailor, Detroit	July 31
Jacob Schlag	Germany, 38	Wagonmaker, Detroit	Aug. 12
John Schlittler	Switzerland, 30	Shoemaker, Detroit	Aug. 5
Abraham Schneiter	Germany, 18	Butcher, Detroit	Aug. 1
John Schubert	Saxony, 39	Blacksmith, Detroit	Aug. 5
Anthony Silva	Put-in-Bay, 34	Sailor, Detroit	July 26
Augustus R. Sink	Germany, 19	Laborer, Detroit	Aug. 11
William W. Smith	New York, 28	Carpenter, Ash	Aug. 6
James K. Soults	Ireland, 39	Merchant, Detroit	July 30
Herman Stehfest	Saxony, 25	Wagonmaker, Detroit	Aug. 5
John Sterling	Ohio, 21	Farmer, Girard	Aug. 2
Alexander Stewart	Canada, 26	Mechanic, Detroit	Aug. 7
Victor Sutter, Jr.	France, 19	Silversmith, Detroit	Aug. 8
William Thompson	New York, 18	Sailor, Monroe	Aug. 11
Michael Tiernay	Ireland, 23	Foundryman, Detroit	July 23
Hugh E Vanderlip	Niles, 23	Machinist, Detroit	Aug. 11
Lewis L. Wadsworth	Redford, 20	Machinist, Detroit	Aug. 11
Thomas A. Wadsworth	Redford, 18	Tinsmith, Detroit	Aug. 11
David Wagg	England, 35	Laborer, Detroit	Aug. 7
Philip Weitz	Germany, 25	Laborer, Detroit	Aug. 8
Charles Willaird	Germany, 21	Laborer, St. Johns	Aug. 11
Robert Wortley	Canada, 25	Laborer, Detroit	Aug. 11
Andrew Wright	New York, 21	Farmer, Monroe Co.	Aug. 11

Francis Wright	Detroit, 18	Farmer, Wyandotte	Aug. 11
William Ziegler	Detroit, 23	Tinsmith, Detroit	Aug. 4
George Zuich	Germany, 34	Laborer, Detroit	Aug. 4

Company B

RANK AND NAME	NATIVITY AND AGE	OCCUPATION AND RESIDENCE	ENLISTED
OFFICERS			1862
Capt. Isaac W. Ingersoll	England, 50	Builder, Detroit	July 26
1st Lt. Wm. H. Rexford	Napoleon, 26	Lawyer, Detroit	July 26
2d Lt. F. Augustus Buhl	Detroit, 19	Student, Detroit	July 26
SERGEANTS			
1. John Witherspoon	Canada, 22	Printer, Detroit	July 24
2. Andrew J. Price	Detroit, 25	Plumber, Detroit	July 24
3. George H. Pinkney	Pennsylvania, 29	Molder, Wyandotte	Aug. 12
4. John J. Duryea	Long Island, 21	Printer, Detroit	July 24
5. George Cline	Germany, 29	Cigarmaker, Detroit	July 24
CORPORALS			
1. Martin L. Peavy	New York, 29	Cooper, Detroit	Aug. 1
2. Robert Gibbons	New York, 23	Printer, Detroit	July 24
3. James R. Havens	N. Hampshire, 35	Joiner, Trenton	Aug. 2
4. Chas. H. McConnell	Ireland, 21	Printer, Detroit	July 24
5. John M. Reed	Ohio, 29	Cigarmaker, Detroit	July 25
6. Samuel W. Church	Dexter, 23	Printer, Detroit	July 24
7. James S. Booth	Canada, 20	Printer, Detroit	July 29
8. John C. Alvord	Grosse Isle, 24	Farmer, Trenton	Aug. 9
MUSICIANS			
Herman Krumbach	Detroit, 15	Plumber, Detroit	July 24
John H. Pardington	England, 23	Clerk, Trenton	Aug. 6
WAGONER			
David Walce	Germany, 44	Teamster, Detroit	July 29
PRIVATES			
Duncan S. Alexander	New York, 23	Sawyer, Wyandotte	Aug. 11
Andrew J. Arnold	New York, 30	Blacksmith, Detroit	Aug. 3
Lewis A. Baldwin	Ohio, 31	Farmer, Wyandotte	Aug. 11
Leander Bauvere	Detroit, 24	Sailor, Trenton	Aug. 12
Francis Baysley	Connecticut, 21	Laborer, Wyandotte	Aug. 11
John Black	Scotland, 38	Ropemaker, Detroit	Aug. 9
Asa W. Brindle	Pennsylvania, 22	Clerk, Wyandotte	Aug. 11
Henry Brown	Canada, 19	Foundryman, Wyandotte	Aug. 11

Willett Brown	New York, 25	Printer, Detroit	Aug. 13
Err Cady	New York, 21	Butcher, Trenton	Aug. 9
Edward Carbrey	New York, 27	Farmer, Wayne Co.	Aug. 9
William Carroll	Ireland, 24	Waiter, Detroit	July 26
Edward B. Chope	Sylvan, 22	Painter, Detroit	Aug. 8
Richard Conners	Detroit, 20	Spicemiller, Detroit	July 28
Benjamin H. Conwell	New York, 39	Ironworker, Wyandotte	Aug. 11
Thomas Coope	England, 41	Carpenter, Detroit	July 29
Anson B. Culver	New York, 30	Musician, Detroit	Aug. 12
Clark Davis	New York, 27	Laborer, Greenfield	Aug. 9
Samuel Davis	Detroit, 18	Dairyman, Detroit	July 28
Frederick Delosh	Deerfield, 19	Ironworker, Wyandotte	Aug. 12
John R. Donaldson	Ohio, 26	Ironheater, Wyandotte	Aug. 11
Mathew Duncan	Scotland, 30	Unknown, Detroit	July 24
Edward Dwyer	Ireland, 20	Spicemiller, Detroit	July 28
Oscar A. Eckliff	New York City, 28	Carpenter, Detroit	Aug. 5
Henry M. Fielding	New York, 24	Clerk, Detroit	Aug. 5
William H. Fowler	Canada, 20	Boxmaker, Detroit	Aug. 9
Joseph French	England, 18	Printer, Detroit	July 25
Christopher Gero	Switzerland, 21	Furrier, Detroit	July 24
George H. Graves	Connecticut, 30	Clerk, Detroit	Aug. 8
John Hackett	Ireland, 23	Sailor, Detroit	Aug. 13
Nathaniel A. Halstead	Canada, 20	Farmer, Trenton	Aug. 12
James Hanmer, Jr.	Detroit, 19	Tobacconist, Detroit	July 28
Lionel B. Hartt	Vermont, 30	Teacher, Detroit	Aug. 6
Robert Henry	Ireland, 26	Carpenter, Detroit	July 23
Charles Henson	England, 38	Bootmaker, Greenfield	Aug. 9
Frank Hicks	Wayne Co., 28	Ironheater, Wyandotte	Aug. 11
William Hicks	Ireland, 23	Tailor, Detroit	Aug. 5
George F. Higbee	Connecticut, 43	Sailor, Detroit	July 31
Henry B. Hudson	Michigan, 20	Merchant, Trenton	Aug. 9
Jacob Klinck	Germany, 18	Laborer, Detroit	July 30
Franz Koch	Germany, 25	Baker, Chicago	Aug. 9
Anton Krapohl	Germany, 27	Bookkeeper, Ann Arbor	Aug. 9
Richard Ladore	Ann Arbor, 19	Cooper, Detroit	Aug. 1
William Lloyd	Pontiac, 31	Farmer, Wyandotte	Aug. 12
Joseph J. Lucas	England, 50	Carpenter, Detroit	July 24
Arthur G. Lynch	Pontiac, 18	Farmer, Greenfield	Aug. 2
William W. Macard	Illinois, 41	Fruitdealer, Detroit	Aug. 12
Joseph E. McConnell	Ireland, 18	Printer, Detroit	not must'd
John McCrudden	England, 19	Miller, Trenton	Aug. 6
Terrence McCullough	Ireland, 21	Barkeeper, Detroit	July 29

John McCutcheon	New York, 23	Printer, Detroit	July 29
Henry C. McDonald	Scotland, 29	Farmer, Brownstown	Aug. 13
James McIlhiny	Ireland, 21	Miller, Trenton	Aug. 6
James McKnight	Canada, 19	Chainmaker, Wyandotte	Aug. 11
Arthur Macy	Massachusetts, 20	Printer, Detroit	Aug. 13
Richard Maloney	Ireland, 38	Laborer, Detroit	July 30
Daniel Mara	Ireland, 20	Spicemiller, Detroit	July 28
Patrick Melone	Ireland, 20	Laborer, Dearborn	Aug. 11
Alonzo C. Mercer	New York, 20	Printer, Detroit	July 31
Charles D. Minckler	Germany, 28	Carpenter, Detroit	Aug. 9
James T. Newington	New York, 27	Carpenter, Wyandotte	Aug. 13
Thomas Nixon	Ireland, 32	Farmer, Oakland	Aug. 12
Daniel O'Beere	Ireland, 26	Laborer, Detroit	Aug. 11
Timothy O'Connor	Ireland, 18	Ostler, Detroit	July 29
James Pender	Ireland, 19	Ironworker, Wyandotte	Aug. 12
Thomas Potter	Ireland, 27	Farmer, Wayne Co.	July 25
Edward A. Raymor	New York, 30	Molder, Dundee	Aug. 9
David Reed	Ireland, 20	Farmer, Hamtramck	Aug. 9
John S. Rider	Detroit, 23	Mason, Detroit	Aug. 12
James Roach	New York, 29	Cigarmaker, Detroit	July 25
Patrick Shannon	Ireland, 27	Mason, Detroit	July 25
Andrew Simmons	Flint, 23	Engineer, Wyandotte	Aug. 13
William Smith 1st	England, 24	Sailor, Detroit	Aug. 5
William Smith 2d	New York, 22	Ferryman, Trenton	Aug. 11
Daniel Sullivan	Ireland, 27	Mason, Detroit	Aug. 11
Morris Troutt	Canada, 19	Laborer, Wyandotte	Aug. 12
James Tyrill	Ohio, 43	Laborer, Wyandotte	Aug. 11
Lafayette Veo	Canada, 23	Farmer, Trenton	Aug. 6
Henry Wallace	Ohio, 35	Shoemaker, Port Huron	Aug. 11
Jeston R. Warner	Newport, 26	Sawyer, Wyandotte	Aug. 11
Nathan Way	New York, 44	Carpenter, Detroit	Aug. 12
Elisha Wheeler	New York, 30	Cooper, Detroit	Aug. 9
William Williams	England, 30	Weaver, Dearborn	Aug. 12
William H. Wills	New York, 27	Farmer, Wyandotte	Aug. 13

Company C

RANK AND NAME	NATIVITY AND AGE	OCCUPATION AND RESIDENCE	ENLISTED
OFFICERS			1862
Capt. Calvin B. Crosby	New York, 32	Merchant, Plymouth	
1st Lt. Charles A. Hoyt	New York, 35	Farmer, Plymouth	
2d Lt. Winfield S. Safford	Canton, 21	Farmer, Plymouth	July 26

SERGEANTS

1. Charles Westfall	New York, 26	Sawyer, Plymouth	July 26
2. Lucius L. Shattuck	Plymouth, 25	Farmer, Plymouth	
3. Augustus Pomeroy	New York, 25	Farmer, Salem	Aug. 5
4. Willard Roe	Plymouth, 24	Joiner, Plymouth	Aug. 5
5. Asa Joy	Redford, 22	Miller, Plymouth	Aug. 8

CORPORALS

1. Abel G. Peck	Connecticut, 42	Farmer, Nankin	Aug. 6
2. Oscar N. Loud	New York, 28	Molder, Plymouth	
3. William E. Sherwood	New York, 27	Agent, Plymouth	Aug. 6
4. James Gillespie	Plymouth, 25	Farmer, Plymouth	Aug. 9
5. Daniel McPherson	Oakland, 24	Farmer, Plymouth	Aug. 9
6. DeWitt C. Taylor	New York, 36	Carpenter, Plymouth	Aug. 5
7. Clark Eddy	New York, 19	Farmer, Plymouth	Aug. 12
8. Charles Pinkerton	Novi, 22	Farmer, Plymouth	Aug. 9

MUSICIAN

Charles A. Phillips	Maine, 15	Student, Detroit	July 25

WAGONER

Nelson H. May	New York City, 28	Town officer, Plymouth	Aug. 5

PRIVATES

D. Leroy Adams	Plymouth, 28	Farmer, Canton	Aug. 6
Thomas A. Armstrong	New York, 21	Farmer, Livonia	Aug. 9
John W. Babbitt	New York, 29	Farmer, Salem	Aug. 9
Oscar N. Baker	New York, 23	Farmer, Plymouth	Aug. 9
Thomas B. Ballou	Nankin, 22	Farmer, Nankin	Aug. 5
John A. Bartlett	Vermont, 25	Farmer, Canton	Aug. 8
William W. Barton	New York, 44	Farmer, Livonia	Aug. 9
Benjamin F. Brigham	Livonia, 32	Mason, Plymouth	Aug. 5
William H. Brigham	Wayne Co., 21	Farmer, Plymouth	Aug. 5
Forest C. Brown	New York, 25	Farmer, Livonia	Aug. 9
Charles Burr	Plymouth, 22	Farmer, Plymouth	Aug. 5
Charles H. Coggswell	New York, 27	Farmer, Plymouth	Aug. 14
George L. Coggswell	New York, 24	Farmer, Plymouth	Aug. 5
Ammi R. Collins	Flint, 19	Laborer, Plymouth	Aug. 5
Norman Collins	New York, 24	Carpenter, Plymouth	Aug. 6
Edward M. Cory	New York, 37	Carpenter, Plymouth	Aug. 5
Alfred Courtrite	New York, 20	Farmer, Plymouth	Aug. 5
James B. Crosby	New York, 35	Farmer, Livonia	Aug. 6
Roswell B. Curtiss	Nankin, 21	Farmer, Nankin	Aug. 8

Henry C. Dennis	Livonia, 26	Farmer, Salem	Aug. 8
Ezra E. Derby	Nankin, 22	Farmer, Canton	Aug. 9
Charles R. Dobbins	Canada, 18	Farmer, Plymouth	Aug. 5
John M. Doig	Salem, 23	Farmer, Salem	Aug. 8
Charles D. Durfee	Livonia, 20	Farmer, Plymouth	Aug. 9
Edgar O. Durfee	Livonia, 19	Farmer, Plymouth	Aug. 8
Watson W. Eldridge	New York, 19	Farmer, Livonia	Aug. 9
Robert Everson	Maine, 28	Filemaker, Plymouth	Aug. 9
Sebri H. Fairman	Canton, 24	Farmer, Plymouth	Aug. 7
Jacob Farley	New York, 27	Farmer, Livonia	Aug. 9
Samuel W. Foster	England, 25	Farmer, Livonia	Aug. 5
James T. Gunsolly	Plymouth, 18	Clothdresser, Plymouth	Aug. 7
Alfred W. Hanmer	New York, 23	Blacksmith, Plymouth	Aug. 9
Wm. A. Herrendeen	Plymouth, 21	Blacksmith, Plymouth	Aug. 8
Alvah S. Hill	New York, 36	Farmer, Canton	Aug. 5
Charles H. Holbrook	Plymouth, 28	Laborer, Plymouth	Aug. 5
Aiken Holloway	New York, 36	Painter, Plymouth	Aug. 13
George W. Hoysington	New York, 36	Farmer, Plymouth	Aug. 5
George P. Hubbell	New York, 20	Farmer, Nankin	Aug. 9
Hiram W. Hughes	New York, 18	Laborer, Plymouth	Aug. 9
William F. Hughes	Canada, 26	Blacksmith, Plymouth	Aug. 5
Bela C. Ide	New York, 20	Blacksmith, Plymouth	Aug. 8
John H. Janes	New York, 26	Farmer, Salem	Aug. 8
Samuel Joy	Redford, 19	Miller, Plymouth	Aug. 9
Oliver C. Kelley	Northville, 20	Farmer, Plymouth	Aug. 5
William Kells	New York, 20	Farmer, Salem	Aug. 9
George W. Kynoch	Detroit, 27	Farmer, Plymouth	Aug. 7
Andrew B. Lanning	Plymouth, 20	Laborer, Plymouth	Aug. 5
Bristol A. Lee	Plymouth, 25	Laborer, Plymouth	Aug. 9
William A. Lewis	New York, 37	Farmer, Plymouth	Aug. 5
James M. Loud	New York, 32	Laborer, Plymouth	Aug. 5
James McKee	Ireland, 24	Farmer, Plymouth	Aug. 5
William McLaughlin	New York, 35	Mason, Plymouth	Aug. 7
Alonzo B. Markham	Plymouth, 19	Farmer, Plymouth	Aug. 5
John C. Marshall	New York, 31	Blacksmith, Plymouth	Aug. 8
J Calvin Maxfield	New York, 23	Blacksmith, Plymouth	Aug. 8
Joshua Minthorn	New York, 28	Carpenter, Plymouth	Aug. 5
Alfred Noble	Livonia, 18	Farmer, Livonia	Aug. 9
John Passage, Jr.	Plymouth, 27	Farmer, Plymouth	Aug. 8
Samuel W. Phillips	Rhode Island, 21	Farmer, Salem	Aug. 8
Nelson Pooler	Maine, 18	Farmer, Canton	Aug. 5
William H. Quance	Canada, 21	Farmer, Salem	Aug. 9

Ambrose Roe	Plymouth, 22	Farmer, Plymouth	Aug. 5
Charles W. Root	Plymouth, 24	Saloonkeeper, Plymouth	Aug. 9
Roswell L. Root	Plymouth, 21	Bookkeeper, Plymouth	Aug. 12
John E. Ryder	Livonia, 19	Farmer, Livonia	Aug. 9
Joseph A. Safford	Canton, 21	Farmer, Canton	Aug. 13
James S. Seeley	New York, 35	Farmer, Plymouth	Aug. 8
John A. Sherwood	New York, 31	Joiner, Nankin	Aug. 9
George W. Soper	New York, 27	Joiner, Plymouth	Aug. 9
Otis Southworth	New York, 28	Engineer, Plymouth	Aug. 9
David B. Stevens	New York, 19	Farmer, Canton	Aug. 5
Frank T. Stewart	New York, 18	Shoemaker, Plymouth	Aug. 8
Christian Stockfleth	Germany, 32	Laborer, Plymouth	Aug. 7
Ralph G. Terry	Canada, 30	Farmer, Plymouth	Aug. 9
William U. Thayer	Plymouth, 21	Farmer, Plymouth	Aug. 9
Robert Towers	England, 36	Shoemaker	Aug. 7
Abraham Velie	New York, 20	Laborer, Plymouth	Aug. 5
Minot S. Weed	Salem, 18	Farmer, Plymouth	Aug. 9
George R. Welsh	New York, 29	Farmer, Plymouth	Aug. 6
Orson Westfall	Plymouth, 23	Laborer, Plymouth	Aug. 5
William H. Whallon	New York, 27	Farmer, Plymouth	Aug. 13
Alfred C. Willis	Plymouth, 18	Laborer, Plymouth	Aug. 5

Company D

RANK AND NAME	NATIVITY AND AGE	OCCUPATION AND RESIDENCE	ENLISTED
OFFICERS			1862
Capt. Wm. J. Speed	New York, 31	Lawyer, Detroit	July 26
1st Lt. John M. Farland	New York, 27	Teacher, Dearborn	July 26
2d Lt. Charles C. Yemans	New York, 28	Minister, Redford	July 26
SERGEANTS			
1. George W. Haigh	New York, 23	Farmer, Dearborn	Aug. 12
2. Francis Raymond, Jr.	Detroit, 19	Bookkeeper, Detroit	July 24
3. E. Ben. Fischer	Michigan, 21	Clerk, Detroit	Aug. 12
4. Charles A. King	New York, 29	Carpenter, Detroit	Aug. 8
5. George E. Moore	Dearborn, 20	Farmer, Dearborn	Aug. 7
CORPORALS			
1. Orin D. Kingsley	Ohio, 20	Farmer, Romulus	Aug. 13
2. William F. Hicks	New York, 22	Farmer, Wayne Co.	Aug. 2
3. Jabez Walker	England, 27	Cooper, Detroit	July 24
4. George W. Chrouch	New York, 19	Teacher, Dearborn	Aug. 19
5. Joseph Eberle	Canada, 24	Shoemaker, Canton	Aug. 13

6. George W. Segar	Redford, 30	Carpenter, Dearborn	Aug. 4
7. Andrew C. Chamberlin	Ash, 19	Farmer, Flat Rock	Aug. 13
8. William Funke	Germany, 18	Cigarmaker, Detroit	July 24

FIFER

Anthony Thelan	Germany, 29	Tinsmith, Detroit	July 31

DRUMMER

Henry D. Chilson	Huron, 16	Farmer, Van Buren	Aug. 8

WAGONER

John Hamlet	England, 36	Carpenter, Detroit	Aug. 7

PRIVATES

Amos Abbott	Canada, 31	Farmer, Romulus	Aug. 8
John M. Andres	Germany, 22	Blacksmith, Detroit	Aug. 8
Henry Babcock	Canada, 18	Wagonmaker, Canton	Aug. 13
Henry S. Baker	Connecticut, 38	Civil Engineer, Detroit	July 29
James N. Bartlett	Plymouth, 23	Farmer, Nankin	Aug. 13
Peter C. Bird	Romulus, 21	Farmer, Romulus	Aug. 12
Robert C. Bird	Romulus, 18	Farmer, Romulus	Aug. 1
Ludovico Bowles	Bruce, 23	Farmer, Wayne Co.	Aug. 12
Persons H. Brace	New York, 20	Farmer, Redford	Aug. 7
Abram F. Burden	Lima, 20	Farmer, Lima	Aug. 12
Eliphalet Carleton	Canton, 19	Farmer, Canton	Aug. 5
Clark Chase	New York, 37	Laborer, Wayne	Aug. 5
George H. Cheney	Dearborn, 25	Farmer, Dearborn	Aug. 7
Sirel Chilson	Huron, 19	Teacher, Van Buren	Aug. 5
Reuben Cory	New York, 25	Farmer, Romulus	Aug. 12
Orson B. Curtis	Nankin, 21	Student, Wayne	Aug. 12
John Danbert	Germany, 20	Gasfitter, Detroit	Aug. 13
Francis Demay	Dearborn, 18	Farmer, Dearborn	Aug. 5
Richard Downing	England, 35	Farmer, Dearborn	Aug. 12
John Dwyer	Romulus, 17	Farmer, Romulus	Aug. 8
Anthony Eberts	Germany, 20	Blacksmith, Detroit	Aug. 6
Joseph Funke	Germany, 20	Mason, Detroit	Aug. 12
John Groth	Germany, 18	Laborer, Detroit	July 25
Thomas Hall	England, 45	Laborer, Springwells	Aug. 12
William Hall	New York, 26	Farmer, Romulus	Aug. 8
Merritt Heath	Van Buren, 21	Laborer, Belleville	Aug. 13
Frank Heig	Germany, 45	Weaver, Detroit	July 24
Oliver Herrick	Saxony, 21	Farmer, Dearborn	Aug. 4
Almon J. Houston	Ohio, 22	Blacksmith, Wayne	Aug. 2
William H. Houston	Ohio, 19	Blacksmith, Wayne	Aug. 13

Shepherd L. Howard	Massachusetts, 31	Engineer, Dearborn	Aug. 12
William H. Jackson	New York, 20	Laborer, Wayne	Aug. 13
James H. Johnson	Wayne, 19	Farmer, Dearborn	Aug. 5
Jacob Kaiser	Germany, 22	Blacksmith, Detroit	Aug. 11
John H. Kingsley	New York, 23	Farmer, Romulus	Aug. 12
Samuel R. Kingsley, Jr.	Ohio, 19	Farmer, Romulus	Aug. 8
William B. Knapp	New York, 24	Student, Detroit	Aug. 7
Conrad Kocher	New York, 24	Shoemaker, Detroit	July 25
Henry H. Ladd	Dearborn, 21	Farmer, Dearborn	Aug. 7
George H. Land	Canton, 22	Farmer, Canton	Aug. 13
Peter F. Lantz	Germany, 26	Laborer, Dearborn	Aug. 7
James Lindsay	Scotland, 42	Carpenter, Detroit	July 28
Henry H. Mills	Oakland, 21	Jeweler, Bellville	Aug. 12
John Moody	Dearborn, 21	Farmer, Dearborn	Aug. 9
Fernando W. Moon	Van Buren, 21	Farmer, Bellville	Aug. 8
Oliver M. Moon	Van Buren, 23	Farmer, Bellville	Aug. 11
Walter Morley	England, 40	Painter, Detroit	Aug. 15
John Neuman	England, 18	Farmer, Redford	Aug. 13
Wm. T. Nowland	Huron, 24	Farmer, Huron	Aug. 13
Michael O'Brien	Ireland, 23	Farmer, Dearborn	Aug. 6
John Orth	Germany, 22	Cooper, Detroit	July 24
George L. Packard	Wayne Co., 18	Laborer, Wayne	Aug. 13
Henry Palmer	Dearborn, 24	Farmer, Dearborn	Aug. 12
James Palmer	Dearborn, 21	Farmer, Dearborn	Aug. 12
Mason Palmer	Dearborn, 22	Farmer, Dearborn	Aug. 7
Richard Palmer	Dearborn, 21	Farmer, Dearborn	Aug. 12
Theodore Palmer	Dearborn, 25	Farmer, Dearborn	Aug. 7
George B. Parsons	England, 44	Tinsmith, Detroit	July 25
Robert Polk	England, 33	Farmer, Redford	Aug. 2
Alexander Purdy	Dearborn, 19	Farmer, Dearborn	Aug. 7
Lorenz Raizer	Germany, 18	Shoemaker, Detroit	July 25
Henry W. Randall	New York, 22	Farmer, Birmingham	Aug. 4
William M. Ray	New York, 30	Farmer, Canton	Aug. 8
James Renton	Scotland, 24	Farmer, Van Buren	Aug. 11
John Renton	Scotland, 20	Farmer, Van Buren	Aug. 11
Andrew Rich	New York, 19	Farmer, Canton	Aug. 12
Horace Rofe	Grosse Isle, 21	Farmer, Grosse Isle	Aug. 13
George P. Roth	Germany, 37	Tailor, Detroit	July 25
David E. Rounds	Dearborn, 21	Farmer, Nankin	Aug. 12
Charles Ruff	Dearborn, 19	Farmer, Dearborn	Aug. 8
William W. Sands	New York, 26	Carpenter, Bellville	Aug. 11
Peter Stack	Germany, 18	Cigarmaker, Detroit	July 24

John Stange	Germany, 18	Mason, Detroit	Aug. 6
James Sterling	Canton, 23	Farmer, Canton	Aug. 12
Newell Stevens	Canton, 17	Farmer, Canton	Aug. 11
Melvin H. Storms	Chicago, 21	Farmer, Nankin	Aug. 11
Andrew Strong	Germany, 26	Farmer, Dearborn	Aug. 12
Aldrich Townsend	Romulus, 24	Farmer, Romulus	Aug. 7
John B. Turney	Dearborn, 23	Machinist, Dearborn	Aug. 12
Albert A. Wallace	Dearborn, 20	Farmer, Dearborn	Aug. 5
Jesse R. Welch	New York, 28	Carpenter, Dearborn	Aug. 5
George Wetterich	Germany, 24	Laborer, Detroit	Aug. 11

Company E

RANK AND NAME	NATIVITY AND AGE	OCCUPATION AND RESIDENCE	ENLISTED
OFFICERS			1862
Capt. James Cullen	Ireland, 41	Contractor, Detroit	July 26
1st Lt. John J. Lennon	Ireland, 26	Clerk, Detroit	July 26
2d Lt. Malachi J. O'Donnell	Ireland, 24	Printer, Detroit	July 26
SERGEANTS			
1. John Galloway	Ireland, 23	Printer, Detroit	July 21
2. Timothy Finn	Ireland, 23	Printer, Detroit	July 21
3. Patrick W. Nolan	Detroit, 19	Tinsmith, Detroit	Aug. 4
4. Rice F. Bond	Vermont, 32	Jeweler, Detroit	July 23
5. Michael Dempsey	New York, 31	Printer, Detroit	July 21
CORPORALS			
1. Amos C. Rodgers	Vermont, 40	Carpenter, Detroit	July 24
2. John Blackwell	Ireland, 19	Blacksmith, Detroit	Aug. 11
3. Frederick Wright	England, 21	Tailor, Detroit	July 31
4. John Hogan	Ireland, 23	Laborer, Detroit	Aug. 8
5. Michael Finn	Ireland, 27	Gardener, Detroit	Aug. 9
6. John McDermott	Ireland, 21	Plumber, Detroit	July 24
7. Eugene Smith	Sandwich, 19	Blacksmith, Detroit	July 25
8. John W. Fletcher	New York, 18	Engineer, Detroit	July 25
FIFER			
James Kidd	Scotland, 18	Baker, Detroit	July 24
DRUMMER			
Charles E. Pascoe	Long Island, 18	Baker, Detroit	July 23
WAGONER			
James M. Bullard	New York, 41	Shoemaker, Detroit	July 23

PRIVATES

Harvey Allen	New York City, 21	Laborer, Romulus	Aug. 5
Moses Amo	Ash, 19	Farmer, Wayne Co.	Aug. 11
Charles Bellore	Canada, 31	Laborer, Detroit	Aug. 11
Sidney P. Bennett	Michigan, 25	Unknown, Unknown	July 30
Joseph R. Boyle	Ireland, 26	Printer, Detroit	July 22
Thomas Brennon	Ireland, 18	Molder, Detroit	July 23
George Brott	Dis't. Columbia, 40	Shoemaker, Detroit	Aug. 5
William Bruskie	Prussia, 19	Farmer, Nankin	Aug. 5
Thomas Burns	Ireland, 27	Laborer, Detroit	Aug. 14
Michael Cavanaugh	Ireland, 35	Laborer, Detroit	Aug. 2
Lucius W. Chubb	Nankin, 19	Farmer, Nankin	Aug. 5
Patrick Coffee	Ireland, 29	Laborer, Detroit	Aug. 4
Arthur S. Congdon	Sylvan, 23	Farmer, Chelsea	Aug. 13
Patrick Conlon	Ireland, 23	Sailor, Detroit	Aug. 7
Henry Conrad	Bavaria, 45	Laborer, Detroit	July 28
Cornelius Crimmins	Detroit, 19	Boilermaker, Detroit	July 25
Louis Dale	Sweden, 38	Sailor, Detroit	Aug. 4
James Dee	Ireland, 23	Laborer, Detroit	July 28
Stephen Delorme	New York, 24	Painter, Detroit	Aug. 4
Martin Devine	Ireland, 41	Trader, Detroit	July 24
Gilbert A. Dickey (N.C.S.)	Michigan, 19	Farmer, Marshall	Aug. 12
Patrick G. Dollard	Ireland, 28	Varnisher, Detroit	Aug. 13
Owen Donovan	Ireland, 23	Engineer, Detroit	Aug. 18
James Doyle	New York City, 22	Carpenter, Detroit	July 28
Dennis Dryden	Ireland, 18	Blacksmith, Detroit	Aug.11
Alonzo Eaton (N.C.S.)	New York, 26	Clerk, Detroit	Aug. 11
Carl Ellis	New York, 29	Sailor, Detroit	July 26
Thomas D. Ellston	England, 20	Painter, Detroit	Aug. 11
William Floyd	Canada, 26	Boilermaker, Detroit	Aug. 4
John Frank	Detroit, 23	Painter, Detroit	Aug. 5
Patrick Fury	Ireland, 24	Carpenter, Detroit	Aug. 14
Robert Gaunt	Hamtramck, 24	Laborer, Detroit	Aug. 12
Thomas Gibbons	Ireland, 44	Peddler, Detroit	July 25
John Grabriel	Switzerland, 42	Farmer, Wayne Co.	July 31
Lewis Grant	Scotland, 32	Sailor, Detroit	Aug. 4
Joseph Green	England, 18	Musician, Detroit	Aug. 13
Isaac L. Greusel	New York, 18	Laborer, Springwells	Aug. 12
Joseph Hirsch	Ohio, 20	Clerk, Detroit	Aug. 25
John Hunt	Ireland, 44	Laborer, Detroit	July 26

James D. Jackson	New York, 23	Carpenter, Detroit	Aug. 8
Andrew Kelley	Ireland, 22	Baker, Detroit	July 30
William Kelly	Ireland, 22	Blacksmith, Detroit	Aug. 11
Frank Kendrick	England, 32	Sailor, Detroit	Aug. 1
James R. Kernan	New Jersey, 24	Plasterer, Detroit	Aug. 14
Patrick J. Kinney	Ireland, 30	Shoemaker, Detroit	Aug. 16
Frederick W. Kuhn	Prussia, 42	Farmer, Wayne Co	Aug. 6
James Laird	Scotland, 35	Laborer, Detroit	Aug. 8
John Lee	Ireland, 24	Laborer, Detroit	July 26
Evens H. McCloud	Vermont, 28	Cooper, Detroit	July 23
John McGeary	Ireland, 26	Sailor, Detroit	Aug. 1
George D. McGiveron	Ireland, 40	Carpenter, Detroit	July 28
Henry Moynahan	Ireland, 18	Sailor, Detroit	Aug. 5
John Moynehan	Ireland, 32	Laborer, Detroit	Aug. 8
Hugh Murphy	Canada, 23	Carpenter, Detroit	July 25
James S. Murphy	Windsor, 22	Tel. Op'r, Detroit	July 24
Andrew Nelson	Sweden, 18	Farmer, Wayne Co.	Aug. 14
Thomas G. Norton	Detroit, 20	Roofer, Detroit	July 25
George Nugent	Ireland, 25	Laborer, Detroit	July 28
Thomas O'Connor	Ireland, 21	Tailor, Detroit	Aug. 12
Michael O'Neil	Ireland, 22	Tailor, Detroit	Aug. 13
Thomas S. Orton	New York, 26	Printer, Detroit	July 23
Charles Paton	Detroit, 20	Boilermaker, Detroit	July 24
Nelson Pelon	Canada, 32	Shoemaker, Detroit	Aug. 11
William Powers	Detroit, 18	Drayman, Detroit	Aug. 5
John Proctor	Wayne Co., 18	Boilermaker, Springwells	Aug. 11
Robert Reed	Canada, 22	Sailor, Detroit	Aug. 4
John Roche	Ireland, 18	Blacksmith, Detroit	Aug. 8
Garrett Rourke	Ireland, 41	Shoemaker, Detroit	Aug. 11
Frank Schneider	Detroit, 18	Stonecutter, Detroit	Aug. 8
John Schultz	Prussia, 26	Farmer, Wayne Co.	Aug. 5
Joseph Smith	England, 41	Shoemaker, Detroit	July 26
John Southard	New York City, 22	Molder, Detroit	Aug. 9
Thomas Stackpole	Detroit, 24	Farmer, Wayne Co.	Aug. 5
Frederick Stotte	Germany, 34	Laborer, Detroit	Aug. 11
Edward Tracy	New York, 19	Sailor, Detroit	Aug. 12
Joseph Trumbradd	Switzerland, 40	Laborer, Detroit	Aug. 1
Patrick Tunney	Maine, 23	Sailor, Detroit	Aug. 5
William Vent	Germany, 18	Brickmaker, Springwells	Aug. 9
John Walls	Ireland, 42	Cooper, Detroit	Aug. 13
Andrew Waubecq	Germany, 38	Stonecutter, Detroit	Aug. 8

James E. Whalon	New York, 30	Printer, Detroit	July 24
Demain Wheelhouse	England, 36	Laborer, Chelsea	Aug. 13
Erskine Wood	New York, 23	Steward, Detroit	Aug. 14
Henry L. Wood	Michigan, 22	Wheelwright, Chelsea	Aug. 13
James P. Wood	Michigan, 26	Wheelwright, Chelsea	Aug. 13
Frederick Woods	Germany, 18	Teamster, Detroit	Aug. 8

Company F

RANK AND NAME	NATIVITY AND AGE	OCCUPATION AND RESIDENCE	ENLISTED
OFFICERS			1862
Capt. Albert M. Edwards	Maine, 26	Journalist, Detroit	July 26
1st Lt. Ara W. Spraque	Unknown, 41	Detective, Detroit	July 26
2d Lt. Jacob M. Howard, Jr.	Detroit, 20	Student, Detroit	July 26
SERGEANTS			
1. Wm. H. Ingersoll	Detroit, 21	Carpenter, Detroit	July 30
2. Charles Bucklin	Michigan, 30	Wheelwright, Van Buren	Aug. 12
3. John J. Littlefield	New York, 31	Physician, Ash	Aug. 12
4. Lewis H. Chamberlin	Brownstown, 19	Clerk, Ypsilanti	July 24
5. Wm. B. Hutchinson	Detroit, 21	Carpenter, Detroit	
CORPORALS			
1. Timothy O. Webster	New York, 31	Overseer, Detroit	July 24
2. George A. Ross	Michigan, 19	Student, Detroit	Aug. 13
3. Oren S. Stoddard	Pontiac, 26	Tinsmith, Detroit	Aug. 12
4. Andrew Wagner	Germany, 39	Stonecutter, Detroit	July 31
5. Benjamin F. Buyer	Ohio, 21	Boilermaker, Detroit	July 25
6. John J. Sullivan	Michigan, 26	Tinsmith, Detroit	Aug. 15
7. George W. Chilson	Wayne Co., 19	Farmer, Van Buren	July 30
8. Levi S. Freeman	Michigan, 22	Blacksmith, Ypsilanti	Aug. 3
MUSICIANS			
William W. Graves	New York, 36	Painter, Detroit	Aug. 5
Daniel D. Webster	Ash, 18	Farmer, Sharon	Aug. 13
WAGONER			
Patrick McGran	Ireland, 23	Teamster, Detroit	Aug. 13
PRIVATES			
Abram Akey	Canada, 36	Farmer, Ecorse	Aug. 13
August Albrecht	Prussia, 28	Laborer, Ecorse	Aug. 6
Louis L. Beaubien	Detroit, 40	Carpenter, Ecorse	Aug. 13
Anthony Bondie	Ecorse, 32	Laborer, Ecorse	Aug. 13

Daniel Bourassas	Canada, 29	Laborer, Ecorse	Aug. 13
Joel R. Brace	New York, 30	Carpenter, Bellville	Aug. 13
William S. Bronson	New York, 42	Farmer, Wayne Co.	Aug. 13
William Bullock	England, 45	Shoemaker, Detroit	July 24
Edward Burkhans	Bremen, 34	Laborer, Detroit	July 24
James Burns	Ireland, 30	Farmer, Wayne Co.	Aug. 7
Thomas Burns	New York, 26	Sailor, Detroit	Aug. 11
Jasper Burt	Michigan, 27	Farmer, Van Buren	Aug. 6
David H. Campbell	New York, 21	Farmer, Ypsilanti	July 30
Henry Chapman	Scotland, 39	Tanner, Detroit	Aug. 14
Frederick Chavey	France, 25	Farmer, Redford	Aug. 13
Patrick Connelly	Ireland, 29	Brickmaker, Springwells	Aug. 7
Andrew J. Connor	Detroit, 32	Clerk, Detroit	Aug. 5
Amos B. Cooley	Macomb Co., 18	Farmer, Livonia	Aug. 5
Joseph Coryell	New York, 31	Farmer, Olive	Aug. 13
Shelden E. Crittenden	New York, 25	Farmer, Ypsilanti	July 30
John Dougherty	Ohio, 32	Shoemaker, Detroit	Aug. 5
Iltid W. Evans	Wales, Eng., 18	Student, Detroit	Aug. 13
John M. Evans	Michigan, 18	Teamster, Detroit	July 26
Alexander D. Fales	New York, 19	Farmer, Huron	Aug. 13
Francis Flury	St. Clair Co., 39	Painter, St. Clair Co.	July 29
Peter Ford	Ireland, 30	Farmer, Wayne Co.	Aug. 7
William S. Fox	New York, 45	Laborer, Detroit	July 26
Adolph Fritsch	France, 26	Peddler, Detroit	Aug. 12
Charles Gochy	Canada, 26	Laborer, Ecorse	Aug. 13
Edward Gohir	Belgium, 22	Farmer, Wayne Co.	Aug. 4
Joseph Gohir	Belgium, 19	Farmer, Wayne Co.	Aug. 4
Sullivan D. Green	N. Hampshire, 29	Journalist, Detroit	Aug. 13
Charles E. Hale	Romulus, 18	Farmer, Romulus	Aug. 11
John Hartmann	Germany, 38	Farmer, Warren	Aug. 13
Christopher Henne	Germany, 25	Cabinetmaker, Detroit	Aug. 13
Ludwig Herzel	Germany, 26	Laborer, Detroit	Aug. 5
Erastus W. Hine	Ohio, 25	Farmer, Monroe Co.	Aug. 13
Elmer D. Holloway	New York, 45	Wagonmaker, Salem	Aug. 13
George M. Holloway	New Jersey, 44	Wagonmaker, Salem	Aug. 9
James Hubbard	Lenawee, 32	Farmer, Olive	Aug. 13
Charles E. Jenner	Michigan, 21	Carpenter, Van Buren	July 31
Fayette Jones	Vermont, 29	Cooper, Van Buren	Aug. 8
William Kalsow	Prussia, 22	Lastmaker, Detroit	July 24
John G. Klinck	Germany, 30	Baker, Detroit	Aug. 13
Irwin W. Knapp	New York, 19	Farmer, Ypsilanti	Aug. 11
George Krumbach	Germany, 18	Gunsmith, Detroit	Aug. 5

Name	Nativity, Age	Occupation, Residence	Enlisted
Antoine LaBlanc	Ecorse, 34	Farmer, Ecorse	Aug. 13
John McNish	Scotland, 30	Plasterer, Detroit	Aug. 13
Gideon Martin	N. Hampshire, 44	Sailor, Detroit	Aug. 8
John B. Moores	Monroe Co., 20	Farmer, Plymouth	Aug. 14
Norbert Multhaupt	Prussia, 30	Shoemaker, Redford	Aug. 13
Myron Murdock	Vermont, 44	Farmer, Plymouth	Aug. 6
George F. Neef	Germany, 34	Farmer, Wayne Co.	Aug. 6
Isaac Nelson	Michigan, 33	Farmer, Plymouth	Aug. 14
Solomon R. Niles	New York, 42	Blacksmith, Ypsilanti	Aug. 8
Edwin E. Norton (N.C.S.)	Michigan, 25	Clerk, Detroit	Aug. 16
Frank H. Pixley	New York, 18	Farmer, Rochester	Aug. 11
Edwin Plass	New York, 23	Farmer, Ypsilanti	Aug. 8
Royal L. Potter	Vermont, 42	Farmer, Ash	Aug. 4
Charles Raymond	New York, 26	Farmer, Van Buren	Aug. 8
Elisha C. Reed	New York, 40	Farmer, Wayne Co.	Aug. 13
Julius A. Reynolds	New York, 37	Salesman, Detroit	Aug. 5
Joseph P. Rivard	Macomb Co., 22	Farmer, Wayne Co.	Aug. 10
Peter P. Rivard	Macomb Co., 22	Farmer, Wayne Co.	Aug. 10
James Robertson	Ohio, 37	Agent, Detroit	Aug. 6
Albert L. Schmidt	Prussia, 18	Clerk, Detroit	Aug. 13
Henry Seele	Germany, 28	Brewer, Detroit	Aug. 13
James D. Shearer	Scotland, 34	Upholsterer, Detroit	Aug. 6
Frank T. Shier	New Jersey, 19	Farmer, Ypsilanti	Aug. 13
William R. Shier	New Jersey, 22	Farmer, Ypsilanti	Aug. 13
Eugene Sims	Ireland, 18	Farmer, Nankin	Aug. 13
Nathan Smith	New York, 22	Teamster, Detroit	Aug. 8
Theodore Smith	Michigan, 35	Engineer, Bellville	July 30
Willard A. Smith	Newport, 18	Sailor, Detroit	July 24
John Stoffold	Germany, 18	Farmer, Wyandotte	Aug. 13
Abel P. Turner	New York, 45	Music Teacher, Ypsilanti	July 24
Josiah P. Turner	Pittsfield, 28	Farmer, Wyandotte	Aug. 14
Mathew Wehrle	Germany, 44	Clockmaker, Detroit	Aug. 5
Marcus G. Wheeler	Wayne Co., 18	Farmer, Wayne Co.	Aug. 8
Ransford Wilcox	Sharon, 24	Miller, Rochester	Aug. 11
Mordaunt Williams	Plymouth, 30	Laborer, Plymouth	Aug. 12
William K. Yates	New York, 25	Clerk, Detroit	Aug. 13

Company G

RANK AND NAME	NATIVITY AND AGE	OCCUPATION AND RESIDENCE	ENLISTED
OFFICERS			1862
Capt. Wm. A. Owen	New York, 27	Lawyer, Detroit	July 26

1st Lt. Wm. Hutchinson	Canada, 22	Butcher, Detroit	July 26
2d Lt. Geo. W. Burchell	England, 33	Contractor, Detroit	July 26

SERGEANTS

1. George Hutton	Scotland, 34	Clerk, Detroit	July 24
2. Benj. W. Hendricks	Monroe, 25	Farmer, Brownstown	Aug. 12
3. George H. Pettinger	New York City, 27	Carpenter, Detroit	Aug. 7
4. John W. McMillian	Detroit, 21	Salesman, Detroit	July 24
5. Charles H. Chope	Wayne Co., 18	Carpenter, Detroit	July 23

CORPORALS

1. Joseph J. Watts	Maryland, 44	Mariner, Detroit	July 28
2. Wm. M. McNoah	New York, 21	Salesman, Detroit	Aug. 1
3. Joseph O. Thompson	Detroit, 22	Butcher, Detroit	Aug. 1
4. John Tait	England, 36	Blacksmith, Canton	Aug. 8
5. Thomas Jackson	Pontiac, 19	Butcher, Detroit	July 31
6. Thomas Suggett	England, 20	Carpenter, Detroit	July 24
7. Charles H. Owen	Missouri, 26	Engineer, Detroit	Aug. 8
8. George O. Colburn	Vermont, 29	Farmer, Ash	Aug. 12

FIFER

David Blakely	Michigan, 29	Farmer, Sumpter	Aug. 7

DRUMMER

William Young	Detroit, 13	Student, Detroit	Aug. 15

WAGONER

Benjamin W. Pierson	New York, 28	Carpenter, Brownstown	Aug. 12

PRIVATES

Charles F. Allyn	Detroit, 18	Painter, Detroit	Aug. 12
Amos Andrews	Plymouth, 26	Painter, Detroit	Aug. 8
Ernest F. Argelbeim	Germany, 18	Farmer, Wayne Co.	Aug. 7
Wm. A. Armstrong	Oakland, 19	Laborer, Ash	Aug. 12
Theodore Bach	Germany, 18	Peddler, Detroit	Aug. 9
Charles O. Baldwin	Washentaw, 24	Farmer, Ash	Aug. 12
Joseph McC. Bale	New York, 21	Farmer, Ash	Aug. 12
Peter Batway	Ohio, 28	Farmer, Exeter	Aug. 13
Henry Bierkamp	Germany, 22	Farmer, Hamtramck	Aug. 11
Lyman W. Blakely	Huron, 18	Farmer, Huron	Aug. 2
Michael Brabau	Hamtramck, 29	Farmer, Hamtramck	Aug. 9
John Broombar	Germany, 18	Farmer, Ash	Aug. 12
Samuel Brown	Detroit, 26	Farmer, Wayne Co.	Aug. 7
Elias B. Browning	Detroit, 18	Painter, Detroit	July 24

John Butler	New York, 21	Teamster, Detroit	Aug. 12
John Cavanaugh	Detroit, 18	Painter, Detroit	Aug. 12
George A. Codwise	Macomb Co., 25	Farmer, Ash	Aug. 12
John Cole	France, 18	Laborer, Detroit	Aug. 12
Henry Collins	Wayne Co., 19	Farmer, Hamtramck	Aug. 8
Charles Coombs	England, 21	Painter, Detroit	July 28
Henry Crothine	Germany, 23	Carpenter, Detroit	Aug. 9
Charles H. Dalrymple	Pennsylvania, 19	Painter, Detroit	Aug. 12
Edwin Delong	New York, 18	Farmer, Brownstown	Aug. 12
Charles Dennis	New York, 18	Farmer, Brownstown	Aug. 9
John M. Dermody	New York, 18	Sailor, Detroit	Aug. 12
Sidney B. Dixon	Detroit, 21	Musician, Detroit	Aug. 7
Joseph H. Drew	Canada, 36	Mariner, Detroit	Aug. 8
Peter Euler	Detroit, 22	Teamster, Detroit	Aug. 7
Jerome P. Fales	Detroit, 19	Farmer, Wayne Co.	July 24
James Ford	Scotland, 22	Gardener, Detroit	Aug. 7
John Foster	Europe, 18	Farmer, Sumpter	Aug. 7
Garrett Garrettson, Jr.	New Jersey, 34	Farmer, Brownstown	Aug. 12
William R. Graves	Ohio, 25	Wagonmaker, Huron	Aug. 12
Edward H. Hamer	Ohio, 31	Carpenter, Detroit	Aug. 11
Marion Hamilton	Sumpter, 18	Farmer, Sumpter	Aug. 7
Michael Hanrahan	Detroit, 20	Molder, Detroit	July 24
William Harvey	New York, 22	Farmer, Van Buren	Aug. 12
Patrick Hefferman	Ireland, 33	Drayman, Detroit	Aug. 13
Samuel T. Hendricks	Wayne Co., 18	Farmer, Brownstown	Aug. 12
George Hinmonger	England, 22	Farmer, Redford	Aug. 8
Lewis W. James	Ohio, 25	Farmer, Wayne Co.	Aug. 13
Wm. H. Jamieson	Michigan, 23	Laborer, Ash	Aug. 12
William Jewel	Salem, 21	Farmer, Ash	Aug. 7
Edwin Johnson	Michigan, 23	Farmer, Huron	Aug. 7
Charles W. Langs	New York, 22	Farmer, Ash	Aug. 12
Enoch E Langs	New York, 19	Farmer, Ash	Aug. 12
Sam'l T. Lautenschlager	Monroe, 23	Farmer, Ash	Aug. 12
James R. Lewis	Michigan, 18	Farmer, Sumpter	Aug. 7
William R. Lewis	Canada, 48	Blacksmith, Sumpter	Aug. 12
Julius Lezotte	Detroit, 22	Farmer, Wayne Co.	Aug. 7
Peter T. Lezotte	Michigan, 23	Farmer, Wayne Co.	Aug. 11
William H. Luce	New York, 23	Clerk, Detroit	Aug. 7
Barney McKay	Ireland, 30	Laborer, Detroit	Aug. 11
Silas A. McMillan	Detroit, 19	Carpenter, Detroit	July 24
William Malers	Germany, 26	Unknown, Detroit	Aug. 15
Charles G. Malley	Monroe, 22	Farmer, Ash	Aug. 12

Andrew J. Martin	N. Hampshire, 29	Machinist, Detroit	Aug. 11
Charles Martin	New York City, 32	Farmer, Sumpter	Aug. 7
Edwin Martin	Huron, 18	Farmer, Sumpter	Aug. 7
George Martin	Michigan, 21	Farmer, Sumpter	Aug. 7
John Martin	Vermont, 24	Drover, Detroit	Aug. 7
Daniel Munz	New York, 20	Sailor, Detroit	Aug. 1
George Oakley	Detroit, 20	Farmer, Wayne Co.	Aug. 8
Arden H. Olmstead	Ypsilanti, 24	Farmer, Ash	Aug. 12
Douglas M. Page	England, 27	Laborer, Detroit	Aug. 7
John T. Paris	England, 21	Tallow ch'r, Detroit	Aug. 12
Henry Robinson	England, 30	Carpenter, Clinton Co.	July 28
William Scerl	Germany, 18	Cigarmaker Detroit	Aug. 11
Hermann Schultz	Germany, 18	Farmer, Wayne Co.	Aug. 7
John Shoane	Hamtramck, 22	Farmer, Hamtramck	Aug. 9
Orville C. Simonson	New York, 28	Farmer, Burns	Aug. 12
Wm. H. Southworth	New York, 25	Farmer, Ash	Aug. 12
Charles Stoflet	Wayne Co., 18	Farmer, Brownstown	Aug. 12
Jeremiah Sullivan	Ireland, 31	Laborer, Detroit	July 25
John H. Terry	New York, 20	Farmer, Sumpter	Aug. 12
David Valrance, Jr	Monroe, 18	Farmer, Brownstown	Aug. 12
Wm. H. Vannoller	New York, 25	Farmer, Burns	Aug. 12
George E. Walker	Oakland, 19	Farmer, Bloomfield	Aug. 4
Albert Wasso	Germany, 18	Butcher, Detroit	July 25
William Weiner	New York City, 18	Sailor, Detroit	Aug. 7
John W. Welsh	New York, 21	Sailor, Detroit	Aug. 2
Albert Wilford	England, 35	Mason, Huron	Aug. 12
Charles A. Wilson	Detroit, 17	Sailor, Detroit	July 31
George W. Wilson	Detroit, 25	Sailmaker, Detroit	Aug. 11

Company H

RANK AND NAME	NATIVITY AND AGE	OCCUPATION AND RESIDENCE	ENLISTED
OFFICERS			1862
Capt. Warren G. Vinton	New York, 32	Builder, Detroit	July 26
1st Lt. John C. Merritt	Unknown, 24	Mechanic, Detroit	July 26
2d Lt. Newell Grace	New York, 36	Lawyer, Detroit	July 26
SERGEANTS			
1. William R. Dodsley	England, 22	Clerk, Detroit	Aug. 5
2. Everard B. Welton	Connecticut, 22	Exp. Clerk, Detroit	Aug. 15
3. Richard H. Davy	New York, 26	Trimmer, Detroit	Aug. 13

4. Herbert Adams	Maine, 39	Lumberman, Plymouth	Aug. 1
5. John H. Wiley	New Jersey, 30	Carpenter, Detroit	July 24

CORPORALS

1. Robert Simpson	Michigan, 24	Laborer, Wayne Co.	July 31
2. William Hunter	New York, 27	Wagonmaker, Detroit	July 25
3. William H. Hoffman	Jackson, 22	Mason, Detroit	July 23
4. Charles M. Knapp	Rhode Island, 27	Clerk, Detroit	Aug. 11
5. Warren A. Norton	New Jersey, 22	Bookkeeper, Detroit	Aug. 11
6. Charles E. Crarey	New York, 23	Unknown, Detroit	Aug. 13
7. Wm. Featherstone	England, 22	Unknown, Detroit	July 28
8. Augustus Hussey	Massachusetts, 19	Clerk, Detroit	Aug. 8

FIFER

Frederick A. Schaube	Germany, 44	Musician, Detroit	July 26

DRUMMER

David Ferguson	New York, 38	Farmer, Nankin	Aug. 12

WAGONER

George G. Cady	Michigan, 27	Farmer, Oakland	Aug. 7

PRIVATES

Peter Alterman	Germany, 32	Tailor, Detroit	July 25
John Benedict	New York, 21	Farmer, Oakland	Aug. 9
Charles Bills	Romulus, 19	Farmer, Romulus	Aug. 13
Marshall Bills	Romulus, 19	Farmer, Romulus	Aug. 13
Robert E. Bolger	Ireland, 20	Laborer, Detroit	Aug. 13
Anthony Brabau	Michigan, 33	Farmer, Wayne Co.	Aug 7
Dewitt C. Butterfield	Michigan, 27	Farmer, Dewitt	Aug. 9
Barney J. Campbell	New York, 42	Saddler, Dewitt	July 26
James F. Clegg	Canada, 18	Butcher, Detroit	July 29
David Congdon	Michigan, 21	Clerk, Dewitt	Aug. 8
Edwin Cotton	New York, 39	Saddler, Ypsilanti	Aug. 13
Michael Cunningham	Michigan, 19	Laborer, Detroit	July 29
Myron Demary	Michigan, 18	Farmer, Dewitt	Aug. 13
Martin K. Donnelly	Michigan, 22	Boilermaker, Dewitt	Aug. 2
James Donovan	Ireland, 34	Laborer, Dewitt	July 26
Michael Donovan	Ireland, 24	Laborer, Dewitt	July 25
Gilbert Dubuc	Canada, 24	Farmer, Greenfield	Aug. 11
Philip T. Dunroe	Michigan, 28	Carpenter, Greenfield	Aug. 11
Edward Eberts	Germany, 28	Bricklayer, Detroit	Aug. 4
Jacob Eisele	Germany, 40	Carpenter, Detroit	July 31
Edward L. Farrell	Ireland, 26	Farmer, Livonia	Aug. 9
Thomas Fitzgibbons	Ireland, 23	Boilermaker, Detroit	July 30

William Ford	Michigan, 21	Carpenter, Greenfield	Aug. 11
Evi French	New York, 24	Farmer, Ypsilanti	Aug. 9
August Gilisback	Germany, 21	Farmer, Wayne Co.	Aug. 14
Theodore Grover	Germany, 19	Shoemaker, Detroit	July 29
Israel Harris	Kentucky, 28	Cigarmaker, Detroit	Aug. 13
Charles W. Harrison	New Jersey, 22	Clerk, Detroit	July 25
Edward B. Harrison	New Jersey, 20	Brewer, Detroit	Aug. 11
Robt. R. Hermann	Prussia, 45	Physician, Detroit	Aug. 2
Abraham Hoffman	Germany, 25	Cooper, Detroit	July 29
Leander R. Hoople	Ohio, 19	Farmer, Dewitt	Aug. 9
Morris L. Hoople	Michigan, 18	Farmer, Dewitt	Aug. 9
William H. Howlett	Michigan, 21	Farmer, Wayne Co.	July 31
William Ingersoll	Oakland, 23	Farmer, Oakland	Aug. 9
Anthony Jacobs	Germany, 27	Cooper, Detroit	July 28
John R. King	Canada, 21	Clerk, Detroit	Aug. 11
John Langdon	England, 33	Farmer, Hamtramck	Aug. 11
Marquis L. Lapaugh	New York, 24	Farmer, Oakland	Aug. 8
John Larkins	Ohio, 26	Sailor, Detroit	July 25
Van R. W. Lemm	Michigan, 19	Farmer, Dewitt	Aug. 9
Charles E. Letts	Michigan, 25	Farmer, Chelsea	Aug. 13
Dennis Mahoney	Ireland, 23	Laborer, Detroit	July 29
John Malcho	Germany, 19	Coffinmaker, Detroit	July 25
Nathaniel J. Moon	Michigan, 18	Farmer, Dewitt	Aug. 9
William Morgan	New York, 20	Farmer, Dewitt	Aug. 9
Robert Morris	New York, 19	Unknown, Detroit	Aug. 2
Alex. H. Morrison	Michigan, 21	Clerk, St. Johns	July 25
Mathew Myers	New Jersey, 23	Farmer, Livonia	Aug. 9
John Nollette	Canada, 24	Farmer, Livonia	Aug. 13
Ira F. Pearsoll	New York, 26	Farmer, Dewitt	Aug. 13
Benjamin Pelong	New York, 23	Farmer, Plymouth	Aug. 2
John Peterson	Michigan, 21	Laborer, Detroit	July 29
John Powell	New York, 26	Clerk, Detroit	Aug. 9
Edwin J. Ranger	Livonia, 23	Farmer, Livonia	Aug. 13
Jas. R. Raymond (N.C.S.)	New York, 36	Photographer, Detroit	Aug. 13
William F. Reed	New York, 20	Photographer, Olive	Aug. 13
George M. Riley	Michigan, 24	Carpenter, Greenfield	Aug. 11
Richard A. Riley	Michigan, 22	Farmer, Greenfield	Aug. 13
A. Wilder Robinson	England, 18	Laborer, Detroit	July 23
Joseph Ruby	Michigan, 22	Farmer, Wayne Co.	Aug. 11
Nicholas Ruby	Germany, 20	Laborer, Detroit	July 24
P. G. Scanlon	Prussia, 45	Farmer, Wayne Co.	Aug. 8
Joseph Schunck	Michigan, 22	Bookkeeper, Dewitt	Aug. 9

Orlando Scoville	Ireland, 25	Peddler, Detroit	Aug. 13
George W. Severance	Michigan, 45	Baggageman, Detroit	July 30
Robert D. Simpson	New York, 20	Farmer, Wayne Co.	Aug. 13
Albert Sons	Michigan, 26	Carpenter, Chelsea	Aug. 13
Daniel Steele	New York, 19	Carpenter, Dewitt	Aug. 9
John Steele	New York, 18	Farmer, Dewitt	Aug. 9
Samuel Steele	New York, 43	Farmer, Dewitt	Aug. 13
Andre J. Stevens	Vermont, 29	Carpenter, Dewitt	Aug. 9
Charles M. Stickles	New Jersey, 20	Farmer, Dewitt	Aug. 9
Arnold Stowell	Pennsylvania, 32	Farmer, Livonia	Aug. 9
George Teufel	New York, 19	Carpenter, Detroit	Aug. 4
Charles W. Thomas	Germany, 31	Painter, Dewitt	Aug. 9
Frederick Uebelhoer	New York, 18	Carpenter, Detroit	July 24
Elmer D. Wallace (N.C.S.)	England, 18	Clerk, Detroit	July 25
Ferdinard W. Welton	Connecticut, 18	Exp. Clerk, Detroit	Aug. 18
Jacob Whyse	Germany, 34	Laborer, Nankin	July 25
Edward Wilson	Germany, 26	Laborer, Detroit	Aug. 11
William C. Young	Detroit, 15	Student, Detroit	July 25

Company I

RANK AND NAME	NATIVITY AND AGE	OCCUPATION AND RESIDENCE	ENLISTED
OFFICERS			1862
Capt. Geo. C. Gordon	Canada, 29	Lawyer, Redford	July 26
1st Lt. Henry P. Kinney	Unknown, 27	Unknown, Detroit	July 26
2d Lt. John M. Gordon	New York, 31	Shoe trade, Detroit	July 26
SERGEANTS			
1. Wm. T. Wheeler	Maryland, 26	Corn. Merch., Detroit	July 26
2. Abraham Earushaw	Massachusetts, 46	Carpenter, Detroit	July 26
3. Albert E. Bigelow	Redford, 22	Bookkeeper, Detroit	July 26
4. Wm. D. Murray	Canada, 22	Clerk, Detroit	Aug. 5
5. Geo. H. Canfield	Redford, 19	Farmer, Redford	Aug. 2
CORPORALS			
1. William H. Cross	Redford	Farmer, Redford	Aug. 5
2. Silas H. Wood	Canada, 44	Carpenter, Detroit	Aug. 5
3. Pratt B. Haskall	New York, 37	Lumberman, Detroit	Aug. 8
4. Jos. U. B. Hedger	Ohio, 20	Clerk, Nankin	Aug. 8
5. George W. Ormsbee	Oakland, 23	Farmer, Redford	Aug. 4
6. Louis Gautherat	Redford, 26	Farmer, Redford	Aug. 7
7. Ferdinand E. Bates	New York City, 18	Clerk, Detroit	July 31
8. Henry L. Houk	Redford, 21	Farmer, Redford	July 26

MUSICIANS

Francis R. Ward	England, 29	Farmer, Greenfield	Aug. 11
Henry C. Stoddard	Greenfield, 21	Tinsmith, Detroit	Aug. 9

WAGONER

Alonzo E. Anscomb	Redford, 23	Farmer, Redford	Aug. 9

PRIVATES

Ralph Archibald	England, 21	Machinist, Detroit	July 28
Abner D. Austin	Canada, 19	Laborer, Redford	Aug. 2
John P. Barrett	England, 42	Farmer, Redford	Aug. 11
George W. Bentley	Bloomfield, 24	Farmer, Redford	Aug. 4
Hiram Bentley	Genesee, 18	Clerk, Flint	Aug. 5
Frederick Bosardis	France, 18	Farmer, Redford	Aug. 5
Jonathan Briggs	England, 33	Cooper, Detroit	Aug. 11
Peter Brink	New York, 36	Sawyer, Livonia	Aug. 5
John Bryant	England, 18	Farmer, Redford	Aug. 2
Seymour L. Burns	New York, 28	Farmer, Redford	Aug. 2
Jacob H. Canfield	New York, 33	Carpenter, Redford	Aug. 4
George L. Carey	England, 28	Farmer, Wayne Co.	Aug. 9
Luther D. Carr	Vermont, 29	Farmer, Redford	Aug. 11
Wm. Charlesworth	Redford, 21	Farmer, Redford	Aug. 2
Patrick Clarey	Ireland, 16	Teamster, Detroit	Aug. 5
John Clerk	England, 40	Farmer, Redford	July 30
William W. Coon	Redford, 26	Laborer, Redford	July 23
Henry Coonrad	Germany, 40	Farmer, Redford	Aug. 11
Ephraim D. Cooper	New York, 39	Farmer, Romulus	Aug.11
Henry H. Crarey	Vermont, 36	Farmer, Redford	Aug. 11
Samuel F. Cromer	Redford, 23	Laborer, Redford	Aug. 7
Oscar Delong	Wayne Co., 17	Laborer, Detroit	Aug. 4
Charles Devantoy	France, 35	Farmer, Wayne Co.	Aug. 13
John J. Dickey	Maine, 35	Ostler, Detroit	Aug. 7
Wallace P. Dicks	Wayne Co., 18	Farmer, Redford	Aug. 11
John Dubois	Redford, 27	Farmer, Redford	Aug. 11
Alexander J. Eddy	New York, 19	Farmer, Redford	Aug. 6
Jay Ferguson	New York, 26	Farmer, Redford	July 29
Richard M. Fish	Lapeer, 20	Farmer, Redford	Aug. 9
William A. Flynn	New York, 35	Sailor, Detroit	Aug. 9
Oliver Gagnier	Detroit, 21	Farmer, Redford	Aug. 8
George B. F. Gren	Redford, 21	Farmer, Redford	July 28
Cross Harris	Wayne, 22	Farmer, Nankin	Aug. 13
John B. Harris	New York, 23	Farmer, Redford	Aug. 11
Nelson Harris	Redford, 22	Farmer, Redford	Aug. 2

Louis Hattie	New York, 18	Jeweler, Detroit	Aug. 8
Lewis Hawkins	Redford, 27	Farmer, Redford	Aug. 7
Mark Hearn	Wayne Co., 18	Farmer, Redford	Aug. 8
Francis C. Hodgman	New York, 22	Farmer, Redford	Aug. 6
Charles H. Houk	Plymouth, 21	Farmer, Plymouth	Aug. 5
Albertus A. Hutchinson	Redford, 17	Farmer, Redford	July 29
Francis Hynds	Ireland, 18	Mason, Detroit	Aug. 2
Isaac Innes	Wayne Co., 18	Broommaker,Nankin	Aug. 13
James S. Innes	New Jersey, 26	Broommaker,Nankin	Aug. 13
William Irving	England, 18	Trimmer, Detroit	Aug. 9
Peter Jackson	Nankin, 20	Farmer, Nankin	Aug. 11
Alpheus Johnson	Wisconsin, 21	Farmer, Redford	July 31
Isaac J. Kibbee	Jackson, 21	Carpenter, Redford	Aug. 1
Charles A. Kinney	New York, 25	Farmer, Redford	Aug. 2
August Lahser	Prussia, 16	Wheelwright,Redford	Aug. 6
Adolphus Londrush	Detroit, 39	Farmer, Redford	Aug. 6
John Maitrie	Switzerland, 23	Farmer, Redford	Aug. 6
Ernile Mettetal	Redford, 19	Farmer, Redford	Aug. 12
James Mooney	England, 18	Peddler, Detroit	Aug. 5
James B. Myers	New York, 25	Gardener, Detroit	Aug. 2
Eugene F. Nardin	New York City, 24	Carpenter, Detroit	Aug. 5
Alexander O'Rourke	New York, 18	Farmer, Flint	Aug. 11
Byron Pierce	Wayne Co., 20	Laborer, Redford	Aug. 11
Palmer Rhoades	Wayne Co., 19	Farmer, Dearborn	Aug. 7
Gilbert Rhoads	Wayne Co., 26	Farmer, Dearborn	Aug. 7
Wm. J. Riffenbury	Oakland, 27	Laborer, Detroit	Aug. 9
Charles Robinson	Detroit, 17	Butcher, Detroit	July 31
Henry Schindehett	Germany, 22	Sailor, Detroit	Aug. 11
David S. Sears	New York, 25	Farmer, Redford	Aug. 8
Adoiphus Shephard	Detroit, 25	Carpenter, Detroit	Aug. 8
Orville W. Stringer	Livonia, 18	Farmer, Livonia	Aug. 4
John L. Stringham	New York, 29	Carpenter, Detroit	Aug. 7
Charles F. Sweet	New York, 22	Farmer, Wayne Co.	Aug. 2
Wesley A. Thinkham	Ohio, 19	Farmer, Romulus	Aug. 11
Theodore B. Thomas	Pennsylvania, 48	Laborer, Detroit	Aug. 8
Wm. E. Thornton	New York, 31	Corn. Merch.,Detroit	Aug. 7
David M. Tilltman	Genesee, 20	Farmer, Wayne Co.	Aug. 12
John H. Townsend	New York, 35	Farmer, Romulus	Aug. 11
Wrn. Vandervoort	Monroe, 24	Farmer, Wayne Co.	Aug. 11
Rosell Van Kuren	New York, 46	Farmer, Redford	Aug. 11
Cornelius Veley	Wayne Co., 26	Farmer, Livonia	Aug. 5

Henry Viele	Germany, 40	Brickmaker, Springwells	Aug. 8
Jeremiah Vining	New York, 41	Wheelwright, Huron	Aug. 11
James Whalen	Pr. Edward Isl., 39	Farmer, Redford	July 29
Hiram A. Williams	New York, 31	Farmer, Redford	July 28
Henry Wooden	New York, 36	Cooper, Detroit	Aug. 11

Company K

RANK AND NAME	NATIVITY AND AGE	OCCUPATION AND RESIDENCE	ENLISTED
OFFICERS			1862
Capt. Wm. W. Wight	New York, 45	Farmer, Livonia	July 26
1st Lt. Walter H.Wallace	Flat Rock, 23	Student, Flat Rock	July 26
2d Lt. David Birrell	Tecumseh, 23	Druggist, Detroit	July 26
SERGEANTS			
1. Robert A. Bain	Scotland, 19	Salesman, Detroit	Aug. 4
2. R. H. Humphreyville	New York, 29	Carpenter, Livonia	Aug. 12
3. B. Ross Finlayson	New York, 19	Druggist, Detroit	Aug. 7
4. George W. Fox	New York, 25	Farmer, Livonia	July 28
5. Wallace W. Wight	Livonia, 18	Farmer, Livonia	July 28
CORPORALS			
1. Ira W. Fletcher	Taylor, 18	Clerk, Flat Rock	July 31
2. Samuel F. Smith	Brownstown, 26	Farmer, Brownstown	Aug. 6
3. Jerome E. Lefevre	Canada, 24	Clerk, Detroit	July 28
4. James T. Rupert	New York, 30	Unknown, Brownstown	Aug. 6
5. Isaac M. Jennie	Ohio, 26	Carpenter, Dearborn	Aug. 8
6. Sarnuel Johnson	Pennsylvania, 28	Farmer, Livonia	July 28
7. Francis T. Dushain	Detroit, 35	Farmer, Livonia	July 28
8. Thomas Saunders	England, 28	Farmer, Brownstown	Aug. 11
MUSICIANS			
Eli A. Blanchard	Livonia, 18	Farmer, Livonia	Aug. 5
Webster A. Wood	Livonia, 20	Farmer, Livonia	Aug. 5
WAGONER			
Hiram Ruff	Dearborn, 30	Farmer, Nankin	Aug. 12
PRIVATES			
Richard D. Ainsworth	New York, 35	Painter, Nankin	Aug. 8
Orville Barnes	Ohio, 37	Farmer, Livonia	Aug. 7
Franklin A. Blanchard	Livonia, 20	Farmer, Livonia	Aug. 12
John R. Brown	New York, 19	Farmer, Brownstown	Aug. 9
John R. Bruce	New York, 29	Farmer, Nankin	Aug. 2

Andrew Bruthaumpt	Germany, 43	Cabt. maker, Detroit	Aug. 5
Thomas Butler	New York, 19	Farmer, Huron	Aug. 11
Peter Case	New Jersey, 18	Farmer, Brownstown	Aug. 9
Wm. J. Chase	Canada, 32	Farmer, Brownstown	Aug. 2
Martin Cole	Canada, 37	Lumberman, Detroit	Aug. 9
William H. Cole	Canada, 21	Sawyer, Detroit	Aug. 13
Michael Daly	Detroit, 20	Teamster, Dearborn	Aug. 12
Wm. H. H. Dana	New York, 21	Sailor, Detroit	Aug. 8
David F. Delaney	Romulus, 18	Farmer, Nankin	
George H. Dewey	New York, 18	Farmer, Wayne Co.	Aug. 7
August Ernest	Prussia, 18	Farmer, Brownstown	July 31
James R. Ewing	Livonia, 18	Farmer, Livonia	Aug. 11
Joseph Ferstell	Germany, 33	Brickmaker, Romulus	July 28
Fernando D. Forbes	New York, 24	Farmer, Brownstown	July 31
John H. Fryer	New York, 18	Farmer, Nankin	Aug. 8
Charles Gaffney	Greenfield, 19	Farmer, Livoni	Aug. 2
Patrick Gaffney	Greenfield, 18	Farmer, Livonia	Aug. 11
Abner A. Galpin	Dearborn, 18	Farmer, Brownstown	Aug. 2
Albert Ganong	Nankin, 18	Farmer, Nankin	Aug. 8
Eugene C. Gessley	New York, 19	Farmer, Brownstown	Aug. 4
Isaac I. Green	Redford, 23	Farmer, Livonia	July 28
Conrad Gundlack	Germany, 45	Laborer, Detroit	Aug. 2
Lewis Harland	Pennsylvania, 24	Farmer, Livonia	Aug. 11
Charles D. Hoagland	New York, 20	Farmer, Brownstown	Aug. 6
Henry Hoisington	New York, 36	Farmer, Livonia	Aug. 11
Artemas Hosmer	Huron, 18	Farmer, Huron	Aug. 5
Charles S. Hosmer	Huron, 18	Farmer, Huron	Aug. 5
Henry W. Jameson	Green Oak, 20	Farmer, Brownstown	July 31
Jonathan Jameson	Green Oak, 18	Farmer, Brownstown	Aug. 2
Wm. M. Johnson	Pennsylvania, 39	Farmer, Livonia	July 28
David J. Kellar	New York, 18	Farmer, Nankin	Aug. 6
Frank Kellogg	Ohio, 18	Moulder, Detroit	Aug. 1
George Kipp	Huron, 24	Farmer, Huron	Aug. 6
Marvin E. Lapham	Livonia, 19	Farmer, Livonia	Aug. 12
William Laura	Dearborn, 19	Farmer, Brownstown	Aug. 2
James Leslie	New York, 36	Farmer, Livonia	Aug. 5
Barney J. Litogot	Wayne Co., 24	Farmer, Brownstown	Aug. 14
John Litogot	Wayne Co., 27	Farmer, Brownstown	Aug. 11
Elija Little	Canada, 40	Farmer, Wyandotte	Aug. 7
Charles W. Loosee	Monroe Co., 18	Farmer, Brownstown	Aug. 9
Daniel W. Loosee	Monroe Co., 20	Farmer, Brownstown	Aug. 4
William D. Lyon	England, 31	Brewer, Detroit	July 28

Evan B. McClure	Pennsylvania, 23	Farmer, Livonia	July 28
Neil McNeil	Scotland, 51	Farmer, Brownstown	Aug. 2
Chas. E. Maynard	Redford, 19	Farmer, Livonia	Aug. 11
Hiram B. Millard	New York, 37	Farmer, Livonia	July 28
Charles E. Miller	Eaton Co., 18	Teamster, Dearborn	Aug. 8
Francis Miller	Brownstown, 18	Farmer, Brownstown	Aug. 2
Simon Miller	Pennsylvania, 50	Farmer, Brownstown	Aug. 2
Eugene R. Mills	New York, 21	Teacher, Detroit	Aug. 12
Andrew J. Nowland	Huron, 23	Farmer, Huron	Aug. 13
James Nowlin	New York, 70	Farmer, Romulus	Aug. 7
George W. Olmstead	Ypsilanti, 18	Farmer, Brownstown	Aug. 2
Elijah P. Osborne	New York, 20	Farmer, Nankin	Aug. 7
Rovert Outhwaite	Plymouth, 29	Blacksmith, Huron	Aug. 5
John A. Pattee	Huron, 18	Farmer, Huron	Aug. 5
Francis Pepin	Detroit, 19	Carpenter, Detroit	Aug. 12
Robert R. Peters	New York, 28	Farmer, Brownstown	Aug. 4
William Platt	England, 39	Mason, Brownstown	Aug. 2
John J. Post	New Jersey, 27	Carpenter, Brownstown	July 31
Abraham Rathbone	New York, 33	Farmer, Livonia	Aug. 6
Sherman Rice	Huron, 18	Farmer, Huron	Aug. 5
Hugh O. Roberts	Wales, Eng., 26	Farmer, Livonia	Aug. 11
Andrew Smith	England, 29	Farmer, Brownstown	Aug. 9
Lilburn A. Spalding	N. Hampshire, 19	Carpenter, Livonia	Aug. 5
Conrad Springer	Germany, 26	Clerk, Detroit	Aug. 8
Jerome B. Stockham	New York, 34	Farmer, Livonia	Aug. 8
Wilber F. Straight	Nankin, 21	Farmer, Nankin	Aug. 2
Charles A. Sutliff	New York, 22	Farmer, Livonia	Aug. 5
Isaac L. Vandecar	New York, 18	Farmer, Huron	Aug. 5
James Van Houten	Ash, 20	Farmer, Livonia	Aug. 6
Jacob M. Van Riper	Ash, 22	Farmer, Brownstown	July 31
Enoch A. Whipple	New York, 37	Carpenter, Brownstown	Aug. 11
Rusus J. Whipple	New York, 39	Farmer, Brownstown	Aug. 9
Gurdon L. Wight	Livonia, 19	Farmer, Livonia	Aug. 5
David A. Wood	New York, 19	Farmer, Livonia	Aug. 5
Wallace A. Wood	New York, 19	Farmer, Livonia	Aug. 5

Bibliography

Busey, John W. *These Honored Dead.* New Jersey: Longstreet House, 1988.

Catton, Bruce. *The Army of the Potomac: Glory Road.* Garden City, N.Y.: Doubleday, 1952.

Coffin, Howard. *Nine Months to Gettysburg: Stannard's Vermonters and the Repulse of Pickett's Charge.* Woodstock, Vt.: The Countryman Press, 1997.

Curtis, O. B. *History of the Twenty-fourth Michigan of the Iron Brigade.* Detroit: Winn and Hammond, 1891. Reprint. Gaithersburg, Md.: Ron Van Sickle Military Books, 1987.

Hunter, Edna J. Shank. *One Flag, One Country, and Thirteen Greenbacks a Month.* San Diego: Hunter Publications, 1980.

Johnson, Robert Underwood, and Clarence Clough Buel, eds. *Battles and Leaders of the Civil War.* 4 vols. New York: The Century Co., 1887.

Jones, Gordon C. *For My Country: The Richardson Letters 1861–1865.* North Carolina: Broadfoot Publishing Company, 1984.

Nolan, Alan T. *The Iron Brigade.* 1961. Reprint, Bloomington: Indiana University Press, 1994.

Smith, Donald L. *The Twenty-fourth Michigan of the Iron Brigade.* Harrisburg, Pa.: The Stackpole Company, 1962.

Tapert, Annette, ed. *The Brothers' War: Civil War Letters to Their Loved Ones from the Blue and Gray.* New York: The Times Books, 1988.

Index

Italicized page numbers refer to illustrations and photographs.

CORALOU PEEL LASSEN

was born in Michigan in 1930, graduated from Boston University
with a degree in psychology, and taught sixth grade until motherhood
became her full-time career. It was during her teaching years that she
gained an appreciation for the Civil War letters that had been in her
family for generations. The mother of two and the grandmother
of two, she lives with her husband on Cape Cod.